Jazz Improvisation for the Classical Pianist

by Martan Mann

Amsco Publications
New York/London/Sydney/Paris

Front cover photography by John Brennan
Back cover photography by Paul Tumason
Cover design by Andy Nunez of Nuberry Advertising Co.

Order No. AM 83841
International Standard Book Number: 0.8256.1229.2

Exclusive Distributors:
Music Sales Corporation
257 Park Avenue South, New York, NY 10010 USA
Music Sales Limited
8/9 Frith Street, London W1V 5TZ England
Music Sales Pty. Limited
120 Rothschild Street, Rosebery, Sydney NSW 2018 Australia

Printed in the United States of America by
Vicks Lithograph and Printing Corporation

Dedication

*This book is lovingly dedicated as a tribute
to my father*

Joseph Zimmerman

*who was always my greatest
source of encouragement.*

Acknowledgements

My special thank you is to my beautiful wife, **Elizabeth**, for her constant encouragement and help. Also, an extra special mention should be given to **Linda Dean**, of **Artsortium Productions**, for her tremendous assistance in helping me to bring this book to print.

I also want to thank many family and friends who were invaluable support to me. Thank you to **Candiya and Bhroam Mann, Ken Silverman, Raymond A. Clark, John Brennan, Paul Tumason,** all the wonderful members of the **Music Teacher's Association of California,** all of my piano students and piano teachers and to **Music Sales Corporation** of New York for distributing this book to music stores.

Thank you to my wonderful Editors, **Elizabeth Mann, Marlene Nichols, Marilyn Theurer, Cecile Wood, and Kim Venaas.** Also, thank you to **Andy Nunez of Nuberry Advertising** for his invaluable expertise in the final printing of this book and video.

A very special thank you to **Apple Computer** for creating the **Macintosh SE Computer** and the wonderful **LaserWriter Printer.** All the music graphics were created with **Professional Composer** by **Mark of the Unicorn.** The book was prepared using **PageMaker Software** by **Aldus Corp.** The information is stored on a **Direct Drive 80 hard disk** by **Jasmine Technologies, Inc.**

Last but certainly not least, thank you to **Henry Schiro,** manager of **The Garden City** in San Jose, (where I have been fortunate to perform for six years) for allowing the beautiful **Yamaha C-7 Grand** to be photographed for the cover of this book.

Table of Contents

Confessions of a grateful guinea-pig.

I am a classically trained pianist who loves jazz and wants to improvise. For years the only way I could play jazz was to play transcriptions of jazz performances. But I couldn't play what I heard in my mind without writing it out first (hardly a spontaneous, creative experience).

Method books were the first way I attacked the problem. The methods they covered ranged from "do what sounds good" to "practice the following 300 exercises for the next 4 years THEN maybe we'll talk about creative expression".

Private lessons with several teachers of improvisation were equally disappointing and showed that the study of improvisation is still a very widely misunderstood and chaotic process.

Enter, **Martan Mann**.

Judge a performer by how he plays.
Judge a teacher by how his students play.

I got to know Martan first as an extraordinary performer, both classical and jazz. Then at a gathering at his home I had the opportunity to hear some of his students. They were wonderful and I found that most had only been studying a relatively short time. They weren't just playing technically correct "licks", they were conversing using music. This was the key.

I immediately started working with Martan

and found his techniques ideally suited to the classically trained musician. He distills the essence of improvisation and makes it understandable. He teaches improvisation as if he were teaching you to speak a language that, up until now, you could only read. He builds upon a classical pianist's background and incorporates the years of experience you already have with the new skills, techniques and mental set you need to grow from an interpreter into an improviser.

This book is the result of Martan's many years of performing and teaching and will show you how to start improvising, how to build your musical vocabulary and how to build that important subconscious mind-to-hand link (to augment the eye-to-hand link you already have).

If you like jazz and if you want to improvise, this method is the most natural, effective way to learn. It works.

Kim Venaas

Prologue -
A Personal Note

This book, _Jazz Improvisation for the Classical Pianist_, has existed inside of me as a living memento to my many years of taking and teaching piano, flute, and theory lessons, and practicing and performing on the piano and flute. This goes back, I think, to one of my first piano lessons when, at age four, my piano teacher smacked me on the back of my hand with a pencil (as I remember it, I think it was a ruler, or a swagger stick) for placing the wrong finger on the right note (or was it the right finger on the wrong note?). My rather opinionated, protective and physically strong mother excitedly showed her the door. Thus proceeded a long history of battles with my classical piano teachers, regarding the penchant that I had for changing notes, phrasing, entire endings to Mozart piano sonatas, etc. It seems that from day one on the piano, I had this urge, this passion, this obsession with . . . _playing music my own way_. (I know, I can hear the _gasps_ wafting through all of the music teachers in this world.) I could never figure out why would she, the piano teacher, get SO upset because I added a new accompaniment to my Chopin Waltz.

Oh well, after many rocky first years as a classical piano student, I think it was finally decided by my classical piano teacher that I should be banished. So she sent me to my first jazz teacher, a very understanding and very inspiring teacher, **Wilbert Baranco**. (You will notice that I left off the name of my first classical teacher(s). I'm not sure if they would want to claim me as a student.) However, with Wilbert, now I knew that I was home. Even though Wilbert was an accomplished classical pianist and excellent classical teacher, he let me, in fact encouraged me to improvise. I was a pre-teenager then, and for me this was more fun than being turned loose in a candy store.

Wilbert gave me large doses of music theory and started teaching me some standard tunes. He taught me how to harmonize and how to play piano in different keys. Most of all, he helped me analyze classical pieces and showed me how the theories applied to the jazz pieces that I was also learning. I should point out, that due to my then "advanced maturity", I was now playing my classical pieces precisely as written. I culminated my wonderful experience with Wilbert by performing my first solo piano recital at his beautiful home in El Cerrito, California. I would like to mention as an aside, that many years after not seeing Wilbert, I dropped in on him where he was performing in Concord, California, and I played some jazz for him, and felt his pride, as a surrogate father, in my more matured abilities. Wilbert Baranco passed away shortly after our meeting, and I will always be grateful for his inspired direction. This book is dedicated, in large part, to Wilbert.

He suggested that I begin lessons with a man who was a legend in San Francisco . . . **Frederic Saatman**. Freddy, as he was called by his close students, was perhaps my main influence because he introduced me to the more difficult works of Chopin, Bach, and Debussy as well as the more refined elements of jazz. We did extensive work on piano technique and many hours of deep analysis of music theory. Freddy had many of the top classical and jazz pianists studying with him. I spoke with one of his star students, **Dave Brubeck**, who told me that Fred was actually his only piano teacher (he said that he studied primarily music composition with **Darius Milhaud**.)

Freddy taught what he called the French method of piano technique, largely made up of relaxation exercises. I learned about arm rotation and most of all learned to appreciate good tone and good phrasing. He had many novel ideas on music theory and showed me, for example, how to analyze Debussy's music to use in jazz. In fact, Debussy, Chopin and Bach all contribute to my jazz playing today. We were playing primarily Chopin *Etudes*, Debussy *Preludes* and *Etudes*, and Bach's *Well-Tempered Clavier*. During this time, while also studying at San Francisco State University as a music major under **Vladimir Brenner**, I was gigging around San Francisco. This book and my musical life is in large part also dedicated to **Fred Saatman**, who passed away several years ago.

We now segue, in this saga of unfolding piano-hood to Hawaii, where after years of performing as a club pianist, I decided, in 1971, to return to college and complete a B.A. and M.A. in music. The B.A. was achieved in Hawaii while studying with two fine piano teachers, **Harry Wilhelm** and **Peter Coraggio**. I studied with Harry privately and with Peter at the University of Hawaii. Peter, at that time, had a sideline of owning a recording studio called Synergia. He was one of the first proponents of synthesizers. He was a representive for early Moog synthesizers and, as such, gave classes in his monster synthesizers. However, I studied only classical piano with him. This was followed by expert classical training with **Aiko Onishi** at San Jose State University, where I received a Masters Degree in Music.

Following my playing a Masters Recital at San Jose State University, (I played Chopin and Debussy) I decided to study jazz. Since then, I have studied with jazz pianists, **Don Haas, Jonny Parsons, Art Lande, and Mark Levine**. My playing has grown in different directions with each jazz instructor. Currently

I am performing with my jazz group, *Nouveau Jazz*, with my dance band, *L'Elegance* and with bassist **Dave Lario** at the **Garden City** in San Jose. My professional life is also well occupied with writing musical arrangements for vocalists, composing, recording, teaching and writing books.

I think that the main difference between studying classical and jazz is that, in classical you learn to perform the music in the manner that the composer intended. In jazz, you explore yourself, and in so doing, discover what *you* intend. Jazz focuses the attention on the performer rather than the composer. The improviser becomes the composer and relates his compositional desires directly and immediately with the audience. He immerses his mind in his unfolding improvisation/composition and in wonderful moments of inspiration experiences a simultaneous communion with the music, other musicians and the audience.

Classical training helps the jazz improviser to interpret specific styles; to develop skills in phrasing, dynamics, and tone; to utilize both hands; to develop memory, reading and sight-reading skills; and gives him or her exposure to some of the world's greatest music. Jazz training helps the classical player by developing "spontaneity" on the keyboard; by helping the player to experience his or her musical direction; helps develop skills in composition; helps develop knowlege of theoy and musical hearing skills; develops abilities in creatively performing with other musicians.

Now we come to the reason that I wrote this music course. Very simply, I sincerely feel that everyone who knows how to play the piano, should naturally be able to improvise. Being that I have improvised since my early piano lessons, I have experienced "both worlds" and feel that I understand the process of improvisation through the eyes of the classical pianist.

This book is a product of my double life as a classical and a jazz player and as such represents my experiences and training in both areas. In my mind they meld as one, with the result that I enjoy many different wonderful musical experiences.

Can we all improvise? I firmly believe that with the correct blend of musical theory, correct thinking, improvisation exercises, knowing what to hear, persistence and patience, and opportunity to play, *everyone can improvise!*

Introduction

INTRODUCTION TO THIS BOOK

I know that there are many classical pianists who feel that they cannot improvise. I feel this is very unfortunate and unnecessary. We learn to walk and then walk where we want. We learn to drive and drive the car where we want. We play tennis, we ski, we spontaneously act and react our way through each day. It would seem then that if we can move our fingers well enough to play Mozart, Chopin, Beethoven, Bach, etc., we should also be able to move them in response to our heart and our emotions!

Oh, yes, I can hear you all say, "it is easy for you to say, beause you are a natural improviser. But what about us non-improvisers -- aren't we destined to only *read* music?" To answer this, I admit that all of us are more talented in one area or another, this does not negate the fact that *everyone* improvises his way through life every day. We don't have a script.

However, I truly feel that if children were taught and encouraged to improvise as they studied their *first lessons*, then they would quickly become "natural" improvisers. Children love to experiment and love to explore and should quickly learn to improvise with the right approach. The problem is that in many classical lessons, the teacher is not an improviser, and wasn't encouraged to be one as a student, and therefore does not know how to teach improvisation. Improvisation can only be effectively taught by an improviser because improvisation by its very nature is not specific and not easily defined and must be taught as a mental/physical exercise by someone who can do it.

MUSIC IS A LANGUAGE

The most important idea to comprehend is that *music is a language*. I believe that the same area of the brain that allows us to communicate in English and other languages, also allows us to *speak* and *understand* music. Try to remember when, as an adult, you were watching two children converse in a foreign language that you did not understand. You possibly would think that, as the adult, *you* should be the one who understands. However, without this language center in the brain understanding the symbols, we do not understand what the children are saying. Language gives us the way to share ideas using the symbols of words. In music, we share musical ideas through "speaking" music symbols. In jazz, musicians often play with other musicians that they have just met, and then play simply by listening. They improvise and share ideas back and forth. If you want to learn to improvise, you have to study as if you were learning a new language. It takes effort, but it is definitely not impossible.

THE SECRET IS IN THE THINKING

The secret is in the thinking. I can remember, as a child, listening to jazz pianists such as **Oscar Peterson** (my idol), **Ahmad Jamal**, and **Art Tatum**, and wondering how anyone could play like they played. I thought, "Where are all those notes coming from?" It was as if they were speaking a *musical* language that I didn't understand. Then as I began to hear their harmonic structures, it became easier and easier to comprehend their music. Then after listening to **Bill Evans**, I went into harmonic ignorance again; and also again, after listening to **Chick Corea**. With each jazz player, you have to understand how he *thinks* and what *musical language* he speaks. Then, you can speak and understand his music, and eventually play in his or her style.

Also, the jazz performer actually *thinks differently* than the classical performer. His musical perspective is totally different. The classical performer's main attention is toward performing the music with a specific interpretation in mind. The jazz improviser, on the other hand, is creating and altering the music as he plays and therefore is musically conversing freely with himself, with the other musicians in the band, and emotionally with the audience. As he plays, the music pours out of him and he has little time to think. Just as in a conversation, he acts and reacts instantly.

This brings me to the major difference in theory used for the purposes of improvisation: *it must be part of your music vocabulary.* Obviously just learning *about* a language does not give you a complete command of that language. Passing tests on vocabulary or grammar would not necessarily teach you to think, converse and emote in the symbols of that language. Probably, you would have to live in the country where that language was spoken and have the opportunity to speak it often, before you would be able to speak and think in it freely. Similarly, if you have not developed these abilities with your *musical* vocabularly, you will not be able to improvise. The subconscious mind has the ability to use symbols to speak, write, think, and create using language. I'm not sure how it puts this all together, but everyone utilizes the subconscious for this purpose. I think that this is the most basic element of improvising music and the best overall concept to hold onto while studying improvisation.

Therefore, in learning an element of music theory, let's say, the Major Triad, you must practice that theory from every angle imaginable. The Major Triad must be learned in *all* keys, all *registers* and *all* voicings. You must improvise with the Major Triad, compose songs using it, be able to recognize it played by another musician and, most of all be able to think creatively with it. Once the Major Triad is mastered, then you should assimilate the Minor, Augmented and Diminished Triads in the same way. We should start with the easiest levels of theory, learn them completely, and then build from there. Once this process has taken hold in your subconscious, you should be able to begin to "converse" through the medium of your music.

Many jazz students encounter this problem by purchasing all the jazz study books that they can find and then start cramming their minds with jazz harmonies, such as chord progressions, jazz scales, chord voicings, and melodic "licks". This often creates confusion and, because the student isn't mastering each step in a logical order, he never learns to improvise.

There is a basic harmonic foundation upon which the more advanced jazz theories are based. It doesn't work to speed ahead to learn advanced and what is sometimes termed, "outside" harmonies if you haven't thoroughly internalized the basics. The first part of this book deals with this basic foundation of theory. I recommend that you thoroughly learn Chapters One and Two before you move ahead to Chapters Four through Six.

The term "big ears" pertains to a musician who has an ability to hear and experience many harmonic and melodic ideas in his head. This gives this musician the advantage of *pre-hearing* many possibilities before he plays them. He also "hears" the harmonic and melodic ideas that the other musicians are playing. He also has the ability to hear ideas in all keys. I am emphasizing this because so many classical players will try to study improvisation, and because this subconscious hearing process does not come as quickly as they would like, they assume that they are not natural improvisers. Then they give up the study. This is regrettable, because if they can slow down, take their time, and begin to assimilate information in progressive layers, chances are very good that they will easily be able to improvise.

In studying improvisation, *you must take your time*. The subconscious needs time to *assimilate* its information so that the intelligence of the player can be manifested. Once this happens, improvisation actually takes place without much thought. It is a natural expression of the feelings of the performer.

PLAYING BY THE NUMBERS

Now, this is the tough one. In order to hear in all twelve keys, it is vitally important that you learn music by the numbers. You must develop good relative pitch. This is a major difference between jazz and classical players. Classical players read notes and think in terms of letter names, ie. B flat, F sharp. Jazz players think in intervals or numbers. The intervals are universal, they exist in all keys. If you, as a classical player, had learned to think in intervals when first starting out, you would most likely be a good improviser today, and would easily be able to transpose into all keys. If these numbers and intervals are not whizzing around in your brain, you have to start the process *now* of thinking in this manner.

I recommend constantly stopping and reminding yourself (out loud) what intervals you are playing. If you do this over a period of time, pretty soon you will automatically think of your music as numbers and not letters. It will help you also if you will incorporate this thinking into your technical practice as well so that you are practicing many exercises in all twelve keys. A very good example is to practice *Hanon* Exercises in all keys. (Please refer to Chapter Three on technique.)

That is why this book will be easier for the pianist who already plays well. If you do not, I suggest that you study with a good classical teacher for a year or two (or more) to build up your technique and abilities of music interpretation to the level where you can perform reasonably well.

A word about computers: It is extraordinarily easy for a computer to transpose (since it thinks in numbers). In my computer, I can instantly change the pitches of any composition that I record, and if I choose to print it out in notation, I can again change keys or pitches. There are many keyboards (which, in reality are computers), which enable the player to dial a new key, or play a bass line or chord accompaniment. However, if the player relies on these devices, he misses the opportunity to train himself to hear music in numbers. Once the player has the abililty to hear in all keys, his improvisational ability goes way up. Without it, the player probably will resort to habitual "licks" or stale musical ideas. Let's face it, computers are wonderful helpers, but a musician carries his ability within himself, irrespective of the gadgets that he is playing.

JAZZ IMPROVISATION FOR THE *CLASSICAL* PIANIST

This book is dedicated specifically to the *classical* pianist who simply wants to utilize his skills on the piano, for his own enjoyment, in his own way. My heart goes out to the classical pianists who have purchased many books on jazz improvisation only to be flooded with chord progressions, chord voicings, and other information that they do not know how to place in their subconscious. Let's face it, most classical players do not have a background or understanding of the world of jazz. It is a foreign world to them because they have not lived with the music and have not, perhaps, even listened to the music to any great extent. Therefore, when they are presented with mountains of theory, they do not know where to start or how to prioritize their study. Therefore I highly recommend that if you are not very familiar with the world of jazz, that you take a course in jazz appreciation; go to hear jazz performers and listen extensively to jazz recordings. You must be familiar with jazz performers, styles and jazz history to understand the many facets of the music.

This book will attempt to address you, the classical player, from the perspective in which you are now comfortable. The beginning of the book will start with elements that you do understand, such as piano technique and basic theory which will center around the major triad and the major scale. We will start with a general approach to improvisation and work into more specific styles. Later, attention will be given toward interpretation of jazz phrasing, dynamics and tone, etc. This is a book which I sincerely hope will help you achieve your goals and as such, wish that you will leave it on the piano to work on, along with Bach, Beethoven and Brahms.

The exercises are developed in an entirely different way than your usual visit to a piano teacher. These are lessons for the subconscious mind. The subconscious must develop the language of music to the extent that you can play spontaneously and effortlessly. This means that you must continue practicing these exercises, *even though you do not see any immediate results.*

I feel that *everyone can improvise if they apply themselves*, will not be too critical, and will not be too hung up on obtaining specific results. The road to being an improviser is not usually a straight line. The subconscious receives information from many sources, and then synthesizes this information in its own way and its own time. Keep thinking how long it would take for a new language to "kick in" before you were actually thinking, emoting and conversing in it. This will give you a yardstick to understand how long it will take to become a good musical improviser.

Also I want to make a distinction between learning general improvisation skills, and learning specific "jazz" skills. As we begin, (Chapters One and Two) we are looking for the subconscious mind to become familiar with pre-hearing notes or ideas and with being comfortable with thinking while in *motion*. After all, music is always in motion or in a time frame. One of the most difficult aspects of improvisation is just becoming used to this "motion". This is similiar to skiing, bike riding and even, walking. After we are comfortable just making sounds and music while in motion, then we can tackle the specific problems of jazz improvisation.

Another element of motion is rhythm. In studying jazz, you must have a highly developed sense and command over rhythm. This means much more than keeping good time and being able to read rhythmic figures. Every style of jazz has its own rhythmic style. You must apply your classical powers of analysis to duplicate this rhythmic "feel". At first this will possibly be a foreign territory for you, but if you listen and analyze, you will capture the rhythmic feeling. The "Groove Tunes" in Chapter Four are designed to be played over and over so that the rhythm eventually becomes locked into your subconsious. The essence of good rhythm is that it lives inside the performer, it is not pasted on from the outside.

Jazz is a style, or more specifically, many

styles. Please remember, though, that as a classical pianist, you can not expect to *suddenly* learn how to play jazz. Jazz represents more than just a style of music, it is a *life*style and a perspective of thinking and feeling. You must listen to a wide gamut of jazz pianists and, I feel, actually develop an appreciation. Certainly you will not like all styles of jazz, but it is still helpful to even listen to the pianists whom you do not like. I recommend using your car tape player. Record your records and CD's onto tapes at home and listen while you drive. Then *think critically of what you are hearing.* The more you listen, the easier it will be for you to adapt your classical styles of playing to the quite different styles of jazz.

You can get bogged down spending days practicing a certain chord progression without placing it in context by having it relate to a specific style or tune. There are many styles in jazz and accordingly the harmonies used for one style will not always work in another. Classical players are used to studying musical styles from a theoretical, technical and interpretive point of view. Jazz books usually assume that all the student wants to play is today's jazz. I believe that classical players have a wide range of improvisational interests, everything from **George Winston** to **Chick Corea** to Boogie Woogie and it is important to analyze different approaches.

Classical players should naturally bring their own backgrounds to their jazz improvisation. Specifically, I see classical players being more inclined to play solo piano. This is because they are used to playing with both hands, and without bass and drums. Many of you will want to play in the New Age styles because the music is generally fuller, more flowing and more peaceful. I recommend that you listen to the stylings of **Keith Jarrett, Bill Evans, Denny Zeitlin, Clare Fischer,** and **Chick Corea** because of their obvious classical backgrounds. Also, without fail, listen to

Art Tatum, Fats Waller and **Oscar Peterson** to marvel at two-handed piano playing at its finest.

WHAT ARE THE GOALS OF THIS BOOK?

This book is meant to be a bridge between your world as a classical pianist and the world of the jazz improviser. It is designed to give you a "leg up" into this world so that you will be able to begin to understand how a jazz player thinks. You should then be more readily able to pick up a jazz method book or two and really delve into the material. This book is designed to present you with specific exercises to give you an encouragement to start improvising. Improvising is like bike riding, you must be moving to appreciate what it takes to ride.

This book does not give you a lot of specific things to play. There are not many written examples or "licks" for you to learn. There are books which will cover this if you want to learn in this way. However, this is not the way that I teach. I believe that if I present you with specifics, you will have the tendency to play only those ideas. This is not what improvisation is all about. Improvisation is discovery and experimentation. I do not intend to steer you into one area or another. Depending on your personal interests, you can learn by listening and, hopefully, having an opportunity to play with a group.

After studying this book, you should be able to find music in a fake book or on a recording and have the tools to be able to understand what is being played. You should have the knowledge to help create your own stylings and arrangements. Also you should have the means to start improvising, even if only on a C Major Scale. In other words, this book is a start, a practical guide to get you going in the right direction.

In fact this brings us to a major problem that you will assuredly run into, and that is, how do you maintain interest during the period when you are simply playing exercises and not particularly sounding the way you would wish. I don't have an easy solution for this except to offer the advice that you try to find a situation where you can improvise in front of others. For instance if you are a church organist, you might try quietly and unobtrusively improvising during the offering. If you are accompanying a dance class, again you might try short periods of improv. Another possibility exists while accompanying a vocalist or instrumentalist (let's hope he is understanding). Perhaps, the best is to form a combo and start rehearsing together with the hope that you can perform gigs.

Also, I highly recommend the *A New Approach to Jazz Improvisation* series of records by **Jamey Aebersold**. This is a wonderful way to "sit in" with good musicians. It is also a good way to learn standards and jazz tunes. There are also records which help you to master chord progressions and other theories. If you can learn a few jazz tunes very well, then when you march into a local jam session, you can suggest that everyone play the tunes that you know. I will be making specific recommendations regarding these records later on in the book.

While you are learning improvisation exercises, you can also be playing written jazz arrangements. These arrangements can give you the experience of playing jazz stylings and chord voicings. Some of my favorite arrangements have been written by **Oscar Peterson**, **George Shearing**, **Chick Corea** and **Bill Evans**. Of course it is always fun to play **Scott Joplin, boogie woogie, and stride piano books**.

JAZZ TECHNIQUE

In Chapter Three, this book also will discuss the technical aspect of how to play jazz so that it *sounds great*. This is a major mystery to most classical players. They can often read an arrangement by **Oscar Peterson**, but for reasons that they can not understand do not sound anything like Oscar. The answer is to learn a *different* technical approach.

There also are technical approaches to playing in different jazz styles. I liken this to the different dialects within a language. It would be very difficult for an average American to speak Spanish in a Spanish dialect the way that, let's say, a South American would. It is equally difficult for the American to play Latin music with the same Latin flair. In order for him to do so, he would have to have the same subconscious reactions. This is similar to Elisa's training in "My Fair Lady" because she had to change every aspect of her subconscious behavior. This takes a good deal of study and practice. Included here, of course, are considerations of phrasing, dynamics, and touch etc. The classical player, skilled in the different technical approaches to playing Bach, Mozart, Chopin and Debussy should also be able to adapt to the playing styles of **Fats Waller, Oscar Peterson, Bill Evans and Chick Corea**, etc.

Chapter Four introduces you to the blues by presenting the Boogie Woogie style. Boogie Woogie is important because it can be played solo. This allows the pianist to work on elements of blues style, soloing, the rhythmic "groove" etc. The blues is so basic to the feeling of jazz that it is a good starting point.

Chapter Five introduces the student to the development of stylizing a tune. This chapter should show you how to approach any tune to develop it in your style.

Chapter Six is an advanced chapter. This chapter gives many ideas to further develop your jazz skills and jazz arrangements.

MASTERING THIS BOOK

Some thoughts on Studying:

1) While practicing the harmonic theories in Chapter One, go through the improv exercises in Chapter Two simultaneously. Place these exercises firmly into your subconscious so that you can do them easily. Work hard on Question and Answer and Modal Improvisation. Know your modes!

2) Chapter Three on Technique may be studied at any time. Refer to the ideas on "jazz technique" when you are working on Chapters four through Six.

3) In Chapter Four, Foundations of Jazz Improvisation, you will start to develop a jazz "feel". Spend a good deal of time on the "groove exercises" so that they become automatic and easy. Try to attain hand independence. Work diligently on Chapter Four *before* you begin Chapter Five on Foundations of a Tune.

4) In regards to Chapter Five, Foundations of a Tune, after working on Eliza, try picking different tunes of varying styles out of a fake book. Remember to learn the tune in *many* ways, from all angles. Make up an arrangement with an intro, the tune, a couple of choruses of improvisation over the chord changes, the restatement of the tune and ending. Even though you are working on Chapter Five, on development of a tune, continue your mastery of the earlier chapters. Do not

begin Chapter Six, Advanced Theory, until Chapters Four and Five are well under way and you feel comfortable with the tune, *Eliza* and other tunes of your own choice.

5) Chapter Six on Advanced Theory will demand persistance because there are so many complex harmonic ideas. Remember that you should pick one or two ideas that you want to work on and try to learn them thoroughly. Then add this new knowledge into your piano arrangements. Do not try to take on too much. Experiment and use your imagination - let the subconscious work its magic. Continue studying the earlier chapters while you are working on the advanced exercises. Apply Chapter Six principles to the tunes you are working on.

6) Do not forget the listening exercises given throughout the book.

7) Keep a Notebook. I recommend keeping a notebook with your reactions to various pianists and jazz styles and why you like or do not like them. In fact this notebook should have several divisions to it. There should be a section of tunes that you are working on. Also you might want to start a section of favorite "licks", or jazz ideas that you learn from records. You might want to have a section of harmonic ideas that you discover from various sources. This notebook can grow with you through the years and, of course, will expand into areas in which you become interested.

8) Don't forget to fill out the Reviews at the end of each chapter! This will help to remind you to organize your subconscious mind.

Remember the purpose of this book, *Jazz Improvisation for the Classical Pianist*, is not to have you sounding like any particular pianist. Even though you

may have your favorite pianist, *you must sound like you.*
Certainly, you as a classical pianist, will bring your own
special feel to the jazz areas. Make your own stamp. *Be
yourself!*

This book is dedicated to having **fun** with
music. *Good luck!*

_____

1 Foundations of Improvisation

LET'S BEGIN!

1. KEY SIGNATURES

You'll never guess where we are starting . . . *Key Signatures*. I know you probably know them, but for those of you who have let some of the information slip away, here they are again. This information must be an active part of your memory because the structure of Keys is a basic framework for the subconscious to refer to when improvising. You should be able to quickly say how many sharps or flats belong to a particular key and then say what the sharps or flats are, and in what order. I recommend that you practice saying the row of sharps and flats (say from left to right) often until it is automatic. Also it is recommended that you write the key signatures being careful to place the sharps or flats on the correct lines or spaces.

A Key Signature can refer to either a *major key* or a *relative minor* key. The relative minor is found by counting six notes up the scale from the root of the major. For example, the relative minor of C major is A minor and the relative minor of F major is D minor. **(See Example 1-1)**

Practice saying the *order* of Flats and Sharps quickly, so that you can instantly know which flats or sharps are in a particular key, and in which order as you write them in the key signature. Simply count down ("across" in the example) the row of flats or sharps in the order that they are presented. For instance, since

EXAMPLE 1-1 - KEY SIGNATURES

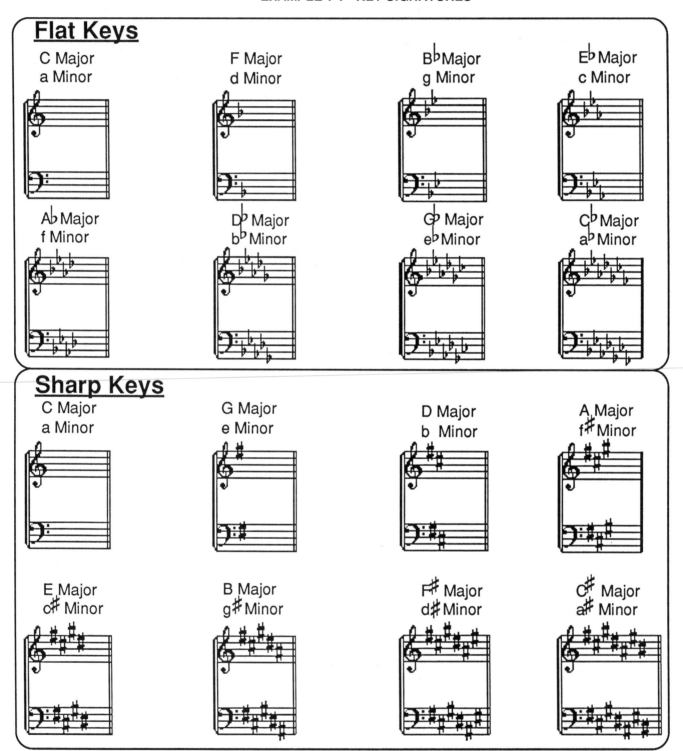

the key "G" has one sharp, stop on the F#, but the key "B" would require that you count down (across) the row five sharps, including: F#,C#,G#,D#,A#. Please note that the sharp and flat rows are in the reverse order of each other. It is also recommended that you *write* the Key Signatures, taking care to place the flats and sharps on the correct lines and spaces. **(See Example 1-2)**

EXAMPLE 1-2 - ORDER OF FLATS

Memorize the <u>Row of Flats</u> so that you can quickly say them.
B E A D G C F

Memorize the <u>Row of Sharps</u> so that you can quickly say them.
F C G D A E B

To repeat: It is of primary importance to completely learn the major and minor key signatures. You should instantly know:

1.) how many flats or sharps are in a major or minor key signature;
2.) which flats or sharps they are;
3.) what order they are written; and
4.) how to write them on the staff.

2. SPELLING SCALES

It is recommended that you are able to quickly *spell* your Major Scales (major for now, minor scales later). This helps in giving you a basis of harmonic analyzation. The following is a method that I learned from **Frederic Saatman** years ago. It is easy and logical. To understand this method of spelling scales you should first understand that all major scales have a half step between steps 3 & 4 and 7 & 8. **(See Example 1-3)**

EXAMPLE 1-3 - MAJOR SCALE

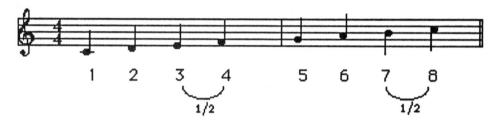

1   2   3   4   5   6   7   8

1/2   1/2

It is important to note that this formula or template allows you to start on any note and play a major scale. You must, however, follow the exact relation of half steps to whole steps. Now we are learning to think in *numbers* instead of letters, which is an essential aspect of improvisation. If we add a sharp in front of *each* note we have 7 sharps (there are 7 different notes). Therefore it is logical that we spell the scale of C#: C#,D#,E#,F#,G#,A#,B#, and C#. We simply spell the scale of C Major and insert a Sharp after each letter. The scale of C♭ is spelled in the same manner. Therefore we could diagram scales starting with the letter "C" in the following way:.

C# - 7#
C - 0
C♭ - 7♭

Now, this method of thinking can be applied to the most other scales. For instance, the scale of F has one flat, B♭. Since, when reading in the key of F, we always look for B♭s, why can this not also work for the key of F#, since *all* of the notes are raised or sharped except the B, which in the key of F was lowered or flatted. So in the key of F#, you *sharp every note except for B, which is played as a natural.* Also, this is another way of knowing that F# has 6 sharps, because if there are seven notes in the Major Scale and one of them is flatted (in the key of F), then it follows that the key of F# would have 6 sharps (since 1 from 7 is six). In terms of the F and F#, and G and G♭ we are thinking of 1 and 6. D and D♭ and B and B♭, we are thinking of 2 and 5. In other words, if we have 5 sharps, we are thinking of the 2 which are *not* sharped. However, when thinking of the 3's and 4's, since it is almost even, we should only think in terms of the flats or sharps that the keys have. This method helps when reading music. This is the way it looks as a chart: **(See Example 1-4)**

EXAMPLE 1-4 - SPELLING SCALES

$$C^{\#} - 7^{\#}$$
$$C - 0$$
$$C^{b} - 7^{b}$$

$$F - 1^{b} - B^{b}$$
$$F^{\#} - 6^{\#} - B$$

$$D - 2^{\#} - F^{\#} \,\&\, C^{\#}$$
$$D^{b} - 5^{b} - F \,\&\, C$$

$$G - 1^{\#} - F^{\#}$$
$$G^{b} - 6^{b} - F$$

$$B^{b} - 2^{b} - B^{b} \,\&\, E^{b}$$
$$B - 5^{\#} - B \,\&\, E$$

$$A - 3^{\#} - F^{\#}, C^{\#}, \,\&\, G^{\#}$$

$$A^{b} - 4^{b} - B^{b}\, E^{b}\, A^{b} \,\&\, D^{b}$$

$$E^{b} - 3^{b} - B^{b}\, E^{b} \,\&\, A^{b}$$

$$E - 4^{\#} - F^{\#} C^{\#} G^{\#} \,\&\, D^{\#}$$

3. THE CYCLE OF KEYS

The Cycle of Keys, also known as the Circle of Fifths, or Cycle of Fourths, etc., is absolutely essential in the study of jazz improvisation. The aspiring jazz student should endeavor to literally know this Cycle backwards and forwards, inside and out. Jazz players constantly relate to this cycle and use it to memorize tunes, create chord substitutions, and relate other jazz theories to it. As we continue on in this study you should use the Cycle to practice technical and theory exercises. And as mentioned before, when we start learning tunes, you will find this cycle invaluable. **(See Example 1-5)**

You can travel either direction around the Cycle. If you move the direction of the flats, you are moving up four notes in the major scale. For instance, if your starting note is a "C", then you will count up four notes, ie: C, D, E, F. "F" starts the next key. Then continue around the Cycle until you end back at "C". You will notice that at the bottom of the page, there are alternative routes, depending if you are traveling around the flats or sharps. These are called "*Enharmonic Keys*". The enharmonic keys represent two spellings of the same scales played on the piano. For instance, C# and D^b are the same note, but their scales have different spellings. You choose one or the other depending on the direction that you are moving around the cycle.

Cycle of Keys Exercise

1) Start at the lowest "C" on the piano and start moving up the keyboard playing up four diatonic (scale) notes around the Cycle of Fourths (Flat direction). Remember you count up four notes, counting the first and last note, of the major scale. Therefore you will be playing C, F, B^b, E^b, A^b, etc. Keep going until you

EXAMPLE 1-5- CYCLE OF KEYS

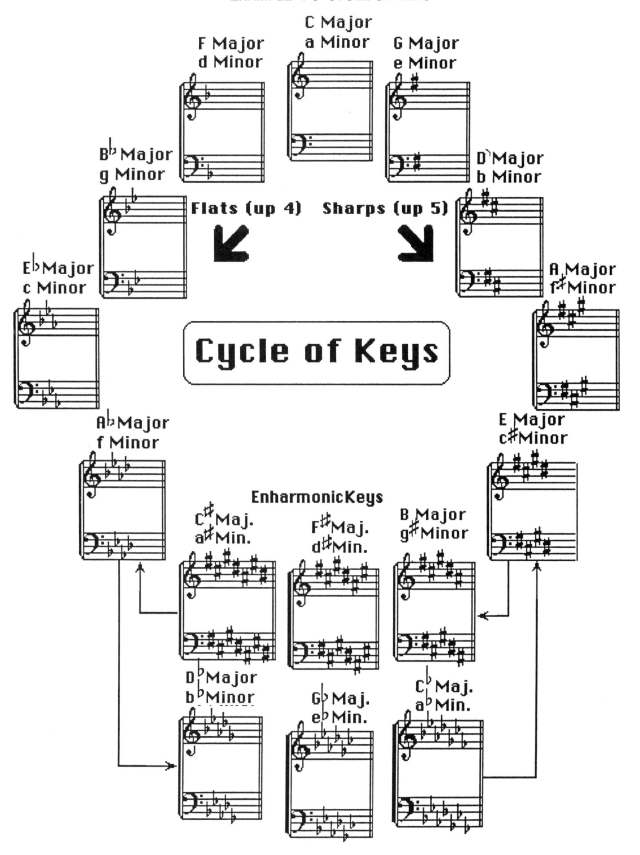

return to "C".

2) Again start at the lowest "C" on the piano and start moving five notes up the keyboard playing around the Cycle of Fifths (Sharp direction). This time you are moving up the keyboard counting five notes up the major scale. For instance, your bottom note is "C", then count up C, D, E, F, G. Then begin on "G" and count up five notes of the G Major scale to "D" etc. Continue all the way around until you return to "C".

3) Now you will note that if you start on a "C" and move up four diatonic notes to "F", you could have also moved *five diatonic notes down* to "F". Similarly, if you move five notes up from "C" to "G", you can also move four notes down to a "G". So you can now practice arbitrarily changing directions as you move your way around the Cycle. For instance, you might move up four notes from "C" to "F", and then down five notes to "B♭", and continue around the Cycle changing directions on the keyboard when you decide. **(See Example 1-6)**

Incidentally, many of the exercises in this book will stress random or spontaneous playing, where you will be making decisions as you play. The idea of this exercise is to familiarize you with the Cycle from either direction, so that you know it automatically.

EXAMPLE 1-6 - UP 4, DOWN 5 (UP 5, DOWN 4)

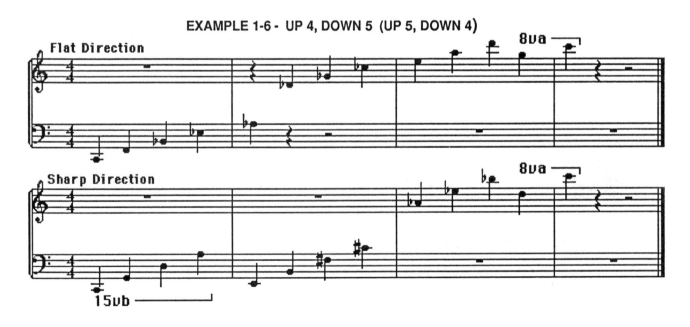

4. FIVE FINGER EXERCISE

This is a simple exercise, but it is designed to familiarize you with thinking in numbers. In fact, this exercise was also used in the Cycle of Keys exercise. The main point about this study is to make sure that you visualize the keyboard in numbers and not letters. As you play think of Whole Step, Whole Step, Half Step, Whole Step. Then you can easily play it starting on any note. Play the five finger exercise up and down chromatically, and around the Cycle of Fourths and Fifths. **(See Example 1-7)**

EXAMPLE 1-7 - FIVE FINGER EXERCISE

5. MAJOR AND MINOR SCALES

This is a good place to suggest that you *completely* learn all your Major and Minor Scales. The best way to think about the Major Scales is in half and whole steps. The half steps are between 3 & 4 and 7 & 8. Practice the scales until you are completely fluent with them. It might also help to practice the scales in contrary motion. **(See Example 1-8)**

EXAMPLE 1-8 - MAJOR SCALES

The Major and Minor Scales can also be learned by thinking in four-note tetrachords. For instance, the major tetrachord has the first four notes of the major scale (whole step, whole step, half step). A Major Scale is comprised of two major tetrachords, separated by a whole step. (See Example 1-8)

For improvisation purposes, it is best to learn the Minor Scales as two tetrachords, lower and upper. The lower *always* has a flatted third. The upper can be learned lowering specific intervals from the Major Scale. For instance, the Melodic Minor has a lowered third in the lower tetrachord and no lowered notes in the upper tetrachord. Incidentally, in classical harmony the Melodic Minor is played with the Melodic Minor on the ascending scale and the Natural Minor on the descending. In jazz theory we usually think of playing the Melodic Minor up and down. The Harmonic Minor lowers the sixth (in the upper tetrachord). The Natural Minor lowers the sixth and seventh. I have included the Dorian Mode as a minor scale simply because it sounds minor and also it is often played in jazz while playing a minor seventh chord.

EXAMPLE 1-9 - MAJOR AND MINOR TETRACHORDS

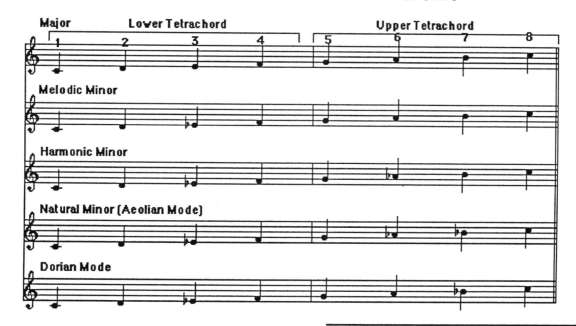

6. INTERVALS

Learning to think in intervals is really the core of improvisation. This enables you to hear in all twelve keys and to play what you are hearing in your head. Classical sight-readers often have a difficult time with this simply because they most often think according to the written notes that they are playing. However jazz players usually have no problem in hearing, singing and thinking in this way. This actually reduces the complexity of music by one twelfth.

The best way that I know to learn to become familiar with intervals is to take them *one at a time* and learn them thoroughly. It is suggested that you start with the diatonic intervals, which are the intervals within the major scale. Then move to the chromatic intervals. **(See Example 1-10)**

A good method to start thinking this way is to find a song which starts with a particular interval. Then use that song to help identify the interval. Remember they should be learned both up and down. Also practice singing the intervals. Simply taking a simple melody and transposing it in all twelve keys will also quickly teach you to think in this way. Everytime you play two notes, either simultaneously, or one after another, think of the relationship between the notes. Don't try to learn all the intervals at once, take time to become familiar with them.

Here are some suggestions to help you to become familiar with intervals:

1) Take a particular interval, for example a perfect fourth, and compose (improvise) a simple composition using only that sound. Composers such as Debussy and Chopin have explored this possibility in their Preludes and Etudes with beautiful results. I

suggest that, since we haven't gone into specifics of starting improvisation, that you begin by exploring the interval randomly in all keys and over the entire range of the keyboard. Then try constructing chords and textures by mixing two of these intervals. (or try three.) Try harmonizing a simple melody using only your chosen interval.

2) After you become familiar with each interval, then start testing your abilities at distinguishing between different sounds. Have a friend test you by playing, for instance, major thirds and minor thirds, or possibly perfect fourths and fifths. This can be done melodically (one note at a time) or harmonically (both notes played together).

3) Take a short melodic idea, three, four or five notes. Analyze the intervals, note to note. Then play this as a sequence, modulating to different keys. Jazz musicians often do this by playing identical musical ideas back and forth.

4) Start now to take simple melodic ideas off of records. Listen to the melody, analyze the intervals and either play the ideas or write them down. (All keys, please!)

EXAMPLE 1-10 INTERVALS

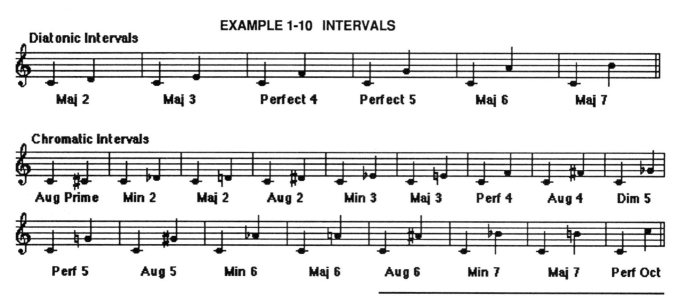

7. THIRDS

Let's start studying chords with the simplest of all, the thirds. There are only two kinds of thirds, the Minor Third and the Major Third. The Minor Third consists of four half steps and the Major Third, of five half steps. It is important to conceive of them in this way rather than by letter names such as "F" or "B Flat" etc. Play these all over the piano taking care to "see" them in intervals. Play them until you can quickly "see" them. Also you want to be able to hear the difference between major and minor. **(See Example 1-11)**

EXAMPLE 1-11 - THIRDS

8. MAJOR TRIADS AND INVERSIONS

The Major Triad is a chord which consists of the root, third and fifth of the Major Scale. If we play it in its root position, the notes, from bottom to top read root, third, and fifth. However if we move the root to the top of the chord, the chord now is in its first inversion. This reads 3rd, 5th, and Root. Again, if we move the 3rd to the top, now the chord is in its second inversion. Practice playing these major inversions until they are *automatic*. As before practice up and down chromatically and around the Cycle of Fourths and Fifths. **(See Example 1-12)**

EXAMPLE 1-12 - MAJOR TRIAD INVERSIONS

9. MELODIC CHORDS

This is a crazy way to add new harmonies into your ears and to master the Major Triad. I warn you, it will sound strange, but the result is that you will start hearing harmonies in fresh ways. This is also a great way to learn the minor triads augmented triads, sevenths or any chords. Also it teaches you to hear a melody in a harmonic way. In other words, if you play a single note melody, the tendency is to only hear the melody note which you are playing. However, implied in that melody note are hundreds, maybe thousands of ways to harmonize underneath it. This teaches you to hear harmonies from the top down.

1) Start with any Major Triad in the root position. Pick a simple melody of your choice (ie: a nursery rhyme) and harmonize that melody using only the root position major triads. The melody will entirely be harmonized with Major Triads. This makes the fifth of the triad the melody note. **(See Example 1-13)**

2) Next harmonize the same melody with the Major Triad in the first inversion. Now the melody note (on top) will be the 3rd of the triad.

3) Now use the triad in the 2nd inversion. The melody note will now be harmonized by the root of the triad. (This exercise can also be practiced in Open Voicings **See Page 45**)

4) Next mix and match any triad in any random order which you choose. This means that any melody note has three possible chord choices depending whether or not you are using the root, third, or fifth. of the Major Triad. (I know, it doesn't sound very musical.)

5) Now you can use Minor, Augmented and Diminished Triads. Randomly mix and match any

way that you want. Do not listen for or expect pleasant sounds or chord progressions. The main idea is to hear new harmonic sounds and to develop quick use of the triads. Then you can use any seventh chord. With seventh chords, you have four possible harmonizations on any melody note **(See page 53)**. Actually, *any* chord can be used in this way.

EXAMPLE 1 - MELODIC TRIADS

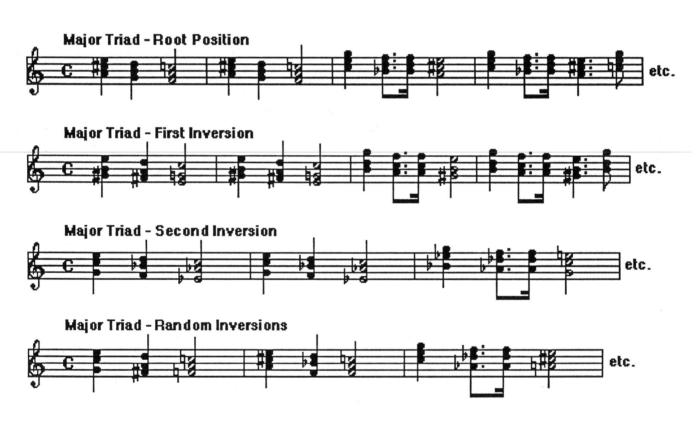

10. ALL TRIADS AND INVERSIONS

Now that we have mastered the inversions in major, it is a good idea to practice them using the minor, augmented and diminished triads. Incidentally, I want to emphasize first practicing the triad exercizes using only Major Triads. The Major Triad seems to have a special place in music theory and should be thoroughly mastered before going on to the other triads. In addition to the Major Triad, there are Minor, Augmented and Diminished Triads. (Actually the Diminished Triad functions more realistically as a seventh chord.)

The triads may be conceived as stacking two sets of thirds on top of each other. Notice that the Major and Minor are opposites. The Major Triad has the major third on the bottom and the minor third on the top, and the Minor Triad has the minor third on the bottom and the major third on the top. The Diminished Triad has a minor third on the bottom and top and the Augmented Triad has a major third on bottom and top. Play these triads in all positions and in all keys until they come easily. Try to learn these chords using the numerical half-step system rather than naming the letters. **(See Example 1-14)**

EXAMPLE 1-14 - ALL TRIADS AND INVERSIONS

11. I - V₇ - I PROGRESSION

The main purpose of studying progressions is to develop good habits of voice-leading. This is important because as you are spontaneously improvising, you do not have time to think about voice-leading, it should be automatic. It is important to practice these progressions in all keys and in all inversions. If you practice them in all inversions you will be able to place any note of the chord on top, thus facilitating more choices in creating a good melody. Please note the way the voices lead to the next chord. For instance, when the I chord is in the root position, the 5th degree stays the same from the I chord to the V chord, and the 3rd moves up 1/2 step and the root moves down 1/2 step. Note how the voices move in each inversion. For the primary purposes of this book, I have given examples of only major and minor. However it is encouraged that you practice progressions using augmented and diminished also. **(See Example 1-15)**

This might be a good place to interject that I realize that the process of assimilation of information takes time. It also takes diligence because of the natural tendency to become frustrated. Also, I realize that you want something to do which will demonstrate the information. However, do not give up the process of assimilating this basic material because as you delve into the later chapters on jazz improv, you will need this information readily available.

EXAMPLE 1-15 - I V₇ I PROGRESSION

Major Triad - Root Position

Major Triad - First Inversion

Major Triad - Second Inversion

10. I - IV - I PROGRESSION

The IV chord moves you one ahead toward the flat direction of the Cycle of Keys. Practice this progression also in all keys as shown and in all inversions. Only the root position is shown in the example. Please note that two options have been given regarding the Minor Triad using the I-IV-I Progression. You can either use the IV chord as minor or major. Of course you are encouraged to try intermixing the augmented and/or diminished triads into your own experimental progressions. **(See Example 1-16)**

EXAMPLE 1-16 - I IV I PROGRESSION

Major Triad - Root Position

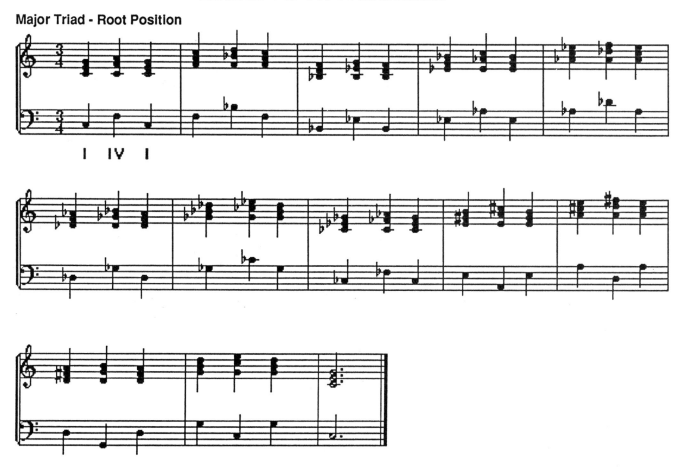

I Minor - IV Minor - I Minor

I Minor - IV Major - I Minor

13.   I - IV - I - V₇ - I   AND   I - IV - V₇ - I PROGRESSIONS

The I - IV - I - V₇ - I progression is a little easier to learn. Practice both progressions in all keys, Major and Minor, and all inversions. **(See Examples 1-17 and 1-18)**

EXAMPLE 1-17 - I IV I V7 I PROGRESSION

EXAMPLE 1-18 - I - IV - V - I PROGRESSION

I Minor - IV Minor - I Minor - V7 - I Minor

I Minor - IV Major - I Minor - V7 - I Minor

14. OPEN VOICINGS

In this exercise we are taking the Major Triad and moving the third of the chord up one octave. Then we are adding another root note one octave up. **(See Example 1-19)** It is recommended that you first practice hands separately, then put the hands together. As with most of these exercises, play in all keys until you are totally fluent. *Fluency is the key to being able to improvise freely.*

EXAMPLE 1-19 - OPEN VOICINGS

15. ADVANCED OPEN VOICINGS

After you have thoroughly mastered the Open Voicings exercise in major, you can move onto the Advanced Open Voicings Exercise in major. Then move on to the minor open voicings. In the Open Voicings Exercise we are playing the open voicings in their natural inversions, but in the Advanced Open Voicings, the main consideration is that you do not double the third (note the exception marked with an *. I have included that only because it was in the original set of Open Voicings.) The only problem with the doubled third is that it has a slightly heavier or more complex sound. If you like that sound, then please use it. Also note that I have organized the voicings according to the intervals in the left hand. These voicings are purely arbitrary, and can be added to if you wish. Avoid spreading the voicings too far apart and be aware that placing a third too low produces a muddy sound. Practice in all keys to develop complete familiarity with these voicings. **(See Example 1-20)**

EXAMPLE 1-20 - ADVANCED OPEN VOICINGS - MAJOR TRIADS

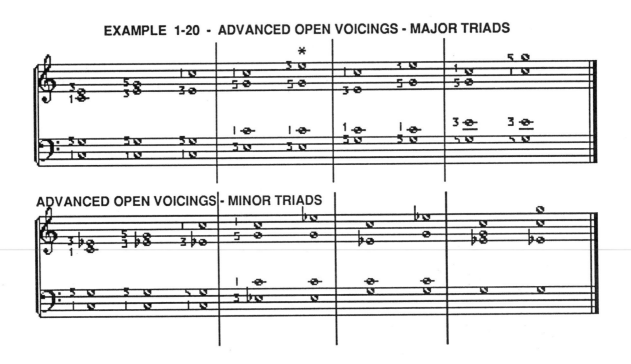

ADVANCED OPEN VOICINGS - MINOR TRIADS

16. OPEN VOICINGS -
I - IV - I, I - V - I, AND I - IV - V - I

Once the Open Voicings have been mastered, then you can begin to play progressions with them. The most common progressions concern the I - IV - I and I - V - I and various combinations of the three chords. It is important to develop an ability to smoothly move from chord to chord without disturbing the inner voice leading. This takes a little practice, but is vitally important in your quest to be a quality improviser. If you develop this ability you can instantly arrange for choir, string quartet, brass and woodwinds, etc. Again, the secret is to be familiar with these progressions in all keys. As you develop your skill at this, you will begin to think more in terms of harmonizing melodies and less in terms of playing progressions as exercises.

The following examples are by no means the only voicings or progressions available to you It is important that you experiment with any voicing that you can think of. Also do not fail to include the Augmented and Diminished Triads into the progressions. The point is that you should personalize the study. Have fun and do not worry about the "rules". Be a child and experience the sounds and emotions. **(See Example 1-21)**

In the upcoming chapter on Basic Improvisation, I will present ideas on using these Open Voicings Progressions.

EXAMPLE 1-21 - OPEN VOICINGS PROGRESSIONS

I - IV - I OPEN VOICINGS PROGRESSION

I - V - I OPEN VOICINGS PROGRESSION

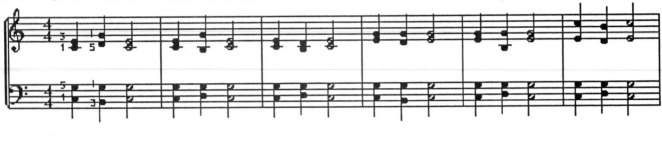

I - IV - V - I OPEN VOICINGS PROGRESSION

I Minor - IV Minor - I Minor OPEN VOICINGS PROGRESSION

I Minor - IV Major - I Minor OPEN VOICINGS PROGRESSION

I Minor - V Major - I Minor OPEN VOICINGS PROGRESSION

I Minor - IV Minor - V Major - I Minor OPEN VOICINGS PROGRESSION

I Minor - IV Major - V Major - I Minor OPEN VOICINGS PROGRESSION

17. SEVENTH CHORDS

In learning the seventh chords, it is recommended that you think in two layers. First think of the triad, which is the foundation of the chord, then think of the type of seventh, which *colors* the chord. This will enable you to hear the underlying basis of the chord and then to identify the type of seventh. **(See Example 1-22)**

EXAMPLE 1-22 - SEVENTH CHORDS

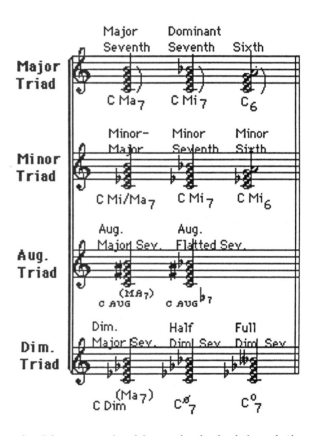

In this example, I have included the sixth chord because it fits the pattern of playing the underlying triad and then placing the major seventh, then the flatted seventh, and finally the sixth. Notice that the sixth is written as a double flatted seventh in the full diminished chord. The diminished seventh chord is especially interesting, and I will develop this subject on the chapter on the Diminished Scale. I recommend, for now, just loosely familiarizing yourself with these sevenths. The following exercise is a good method to learn the sevenths. Of course, it is recommended that you learn one at a time, playing it in all inversions and in open voicings. Later in this book a good deal of discussion will be on the *de-emphasis* of chords. However, it is important that you are aware of their labels and sounds. **(See Example 1-23)**

EXAMPLE 1-23 - SEVENTH CHORDS EXERCISE

After playing the Major Sevenths in different inversions, play *all* the sevenths that you have been given in the same manner.

The sevenths can also be learned in open voicings. **(See Example 1-24)**

The idea is to play all the sevenths chords in both closed and open positions, until you can freely play them starting at any point on the Cycle of Keys. If you want, you can construct a sevenths exercise moving around the Sharp direction of the Cycle, or you can move up and down chromatically. The main object is to fully know the seventh chords.

Visualization

A wonderful mental exercise to practice often is to visualize the next chord in an exercise that you are practicing. Let your hands rest on the bottom of the keys, then precisely visualize the next chord. Note: do not move to the next chord until the visualization is secure. Also do not "hover" over the new chord until you are sure. Simply move directly to the bottom of the keys of the new chord and play it securely. In this manner, you will begin to teach your subconscious mind to think ahead. You will also learn your exercise more quickly this way.

EXAMPLE 1-24 - OPEN VOICING - SEVENTH CHORDS

Flat Direction

Sharp Direction

Sevenths Exercise - Dominant Seventh

Sevenths Exercise - Minor Seventh

18. MAJOR SCALE SEVENTHS

The following is an example of the *Major Scale Sevenths*. These are the natural seventh chords which play up the Major Scale. You should definitely play these in all keys. **(See Example 1-25)**

EXAMPLE 1-25 - MAJOR SCALE SEVENTHS

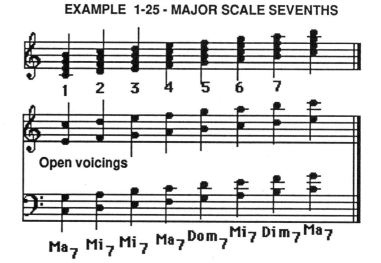

Foundations of Improvisation - Review

KEYS AND SCALES

1)   Do you know the *Flat and Sharp Key Signatures?* You should be able to quickly say how many sharps or flats are in a particular key signature.   **(Example 1-1, Page 22)** Memorize the *Order of Sharps and Flats* so that you can say them quickly. **(Example 1-2, Page 23)** Know the keys in Major and Minor.

Completed: Date_____

2)   Can you *spell the Major Scales* without referring to the piano? **(Examples 1-3, Page 24 & 1-4, Page 25)**

Completed: Date_____

3)   Can you *visualize the Cycle* without looking at it? **(Example 1-5, Page 27)** Can you *quickly play* the *Cycle of Keys* exercises, *"Up 5, Down 4"* and *"Up 4, Down 5"?* **(Example 1-6, Page 28)**

Completed: Date_____

4)   Can you play the *"Five Finger Exercise"* by thinking in numbers? **(Example 1-7, Page 29)**

Completed: Date_____

5)   Can you comfortably play the *Major Scales* with with either hand or two hands? This may take awhile. **(Example 1-8, Pages 29 & 30)**

Completed: Date_____

6)   Can you comfortably play the *Minor Scales* and *Dorian Mode* with with either hand or two hands? This will take awhile. **(Example 1-9, Page 31)**

Completed: Date_____

INTERVALS

7)   Did you take each interval and learn it completely so that you are totally familiar with it? **(Example 10, Page 33)**

Completed: Date_____

8)   Did you find a song to help identify each interval?   Completed: Date_____

9)   Did you compose simple compositions using each interval?   Completed: Date_____

10)   Did you have a friend test your familiarity with intervals?   Completed: Date_____

11)   Did you take a short melodic idea and play in different keys?   Completed: Date_____

12)   Have you begun to transcribe simple ideas off of records using your knowledge of intervals? These ideas should be played in all keys.   Completed: Date_____

CHORDS

13)   Can you *play* both the *Major and Minor Thirds* throughout the piano? Can you *write* them? Can you *sing* them? **(Example 1-11) Page 34)**   Completed: Date_____

14)   Can you *play* both the *Major and Minor Triads* throughout the piano? Can you *write* them? Can you *sing* them? **(Example 1-12, Page34)**   Completed: Date_____

15)   Have you *harmonized simple melodies* with Major Triads in the Root Position, 1st Inversion, and 2nd Inversion and Random Inversions? **(Example 1-13, Pages 35 & 36)**   Completed: Date_____

16)   Can you *play* the *Major, Minor, Augmented and Diminished Triads* throughout the piano? Can you *write* them? Can you *sing* them? Can you harmonize simple melodies with them? **(Example 1-14, Page37)**   Completed: Date_____

17)   Can you quickly play the *I, V7, I Progression* in the Root Position around the Cycle of Fourths; First Inversion; Second Inversion? **(Example 1-15, Pages 38 & 39)**   Completed: Date_____

18)   Can you quickly play the *Minor I, V7, Minor I Progression* around the Cycle of Fourths in the Root Position , First Inversion, Second Inversion, Cycle of Fifths,etc.? **(Example 1-15, Page 39)**

Completed: Date_____

19)   Can you quickly play the *I Major, IV Major, I Major Progression* in the Root Position around the Cycle of Fourths, First Inversion , Second Inversion? **(Example 1-16, Page 41)**

Completed: Date_____

20)   Can you quickly play the *I Minor, IV Minor, I Minor Progression* in the Root Position around the Cycle of Fourths, First Inversion, Second Inversion? **(Example 1-16, Page 42)**

Completed: Date_____

21)   Can you quickly play the *I Minor, IV Major, I Minor Progression* in the Root Position around the Cycle of Fourths, First Inversion, Second Inversion? **(Example 1-16, Page 42)**

Completed: Date_____

22)   Can you quickly play the *I, IV, I, V7, I Progression* in the Root Position around the Cycle of Fourths, First Inversion , Second Inversion? **(Example 1-17, Page 43)**

Completed: Date_____

23)   Can you quickly play the *I, IV, V7, I Progression* in the Root Position around the Cycle of Fourths, First Inversion, Second Inversion? **(Example 1-18, Page 43)**

Completed: Date_____

24)   Can you quickly play the *I Minor, IV Minor, I Minor, V7, I Minor Progression* in the Root Position around the Cycle of Fourths, First Inversion, Second Inversion? **(Example 1-18, Page 44)**

Completed: Date_____

25)   Can you quickly play the *I Minor, IV Major, I Minor, V7, I Minor Progression* in the Root Position around the Cycle of Fourths, First Inversion, Second Inversion? **(Example 1-18, Page 44)**

Completed: Date_____

26) Can you play the *Open Voicings* in all keys in Major and Minor? **(Example 1-19, Page 45)**

Completed: Date_____

27) Can you play the *Advanced Open Voicings* in all keys in Major and Minor? **(Example 1-20, Page 46)**

Completed: Date_____

28) Can you play the *I, IV, I Advanced Open Voicings* in all keys? **(Example 1-21, Page 47)**

Completed: Date_____

29) Can you play the *I, V, I Advanced Open Voicings* in all keys? **(Example 1-21, Page 48)**

Completed: Date_____

30) Can you play the *I, IV, V, I Advanced Open Voicings* in all keys? **(Example 1-21, Page 48)**

Completed: Date_____

31) Can you play the *I Minor, IV Minor, I Minor Advanced Open Voicings* in all keys? **(Example 1-21, Page 49)**

Completed: Date_____

32) Can you play the *I Minor, IV Major, I Minor Advanced Open Voicings* in all keys? **(Example 1-21, Page 49)**

Completed: Date_____

33) Can you play the *I Minor, V Major, I Minor Advanced Open Voicings* in all keys? **(Example 1-21, Page 50)**

Completed: Date_____

34) Can you play the *I Minor, IV Minor, V Major, I Minor Advanced Open Voicings* in all keys? **(Example 1-21, Page 51)**

Completed: Date_____

35) Can you play the *I Minor, IV Major, V Major, I Minor Advanced Open Voicings* in all keys in Major and Minor? **(Example 1-21, Page 52)**

Completed: Date_____

SEVENTH CHORDS

36) Study chart on **Example 1-22, Page 53**. Do you see the relationship of the type of triad with the type of

seventh?

Completed: Date_____

37)   Practice the *Sevenths Chord Exercise* **(Example 1-23, Page 54)** in all keys and all inversions. Practice in the following sevenths:

    a)   Major Seventh
    b)   Dominant Seventh
    c)   Major Sixth
    d)   Minor Triad with Major Seventh
    e)   Minor Seventh
    f)   Minor Sixth
    g)   Augmented with Major Seventh
    h)   Augmented with Flatted Seventh
    i)   Diminished with Major Seventh
    j)   Diminished with Flatted Seventh (Also known as a Half Diminished or Minor Seventh with Flatted Fifth)
    k)   Diminished Seventh

Have you practiced the *Seventh Chords Exercise* in all the types of sevenths and in all keys and inversions and in open voicings? This *will* take awhile!

Completed: Date_____

38)   Have you practiced the *Visualization Exercise*? **(Page 55)**

Completed: Date_____

39)   Have you practiced the *Major Scale Sevenths* Exercise. This should be practiced in all keys. **(Example 1-25, Page 59)**

Completed: Date_____

Note:

    This chapter can not be assimilated quickly. You must have a practice routine. The next chapter, Beginning Improvisation is designed to be practiced along with this chapter. Take your time.

2 Beginning Improvisation

19. QUESTION & ANSWER

Question and Answer solves the problem: How do I begin to improvise? Improvising is a lot like skiing. If you stand at the top of the hill without pushing off, you never know the experience of coming down the hill. We often stare at the piano, waiting for an idea to strike us before we start improvising, and never get started. More than any other factor, just learning where and how to *start* is most important.

To begin with, the very nature of improvising demands that you have *basic elements*. Then, the challenge is to change those elements. For example, you can improvise from a melodic idea, or a rhythmic idea, or a chord pattern, or even a "sound effect". The main issue is to set up some parameters that will serve as the basis for the improvisation.

In jazz, improvisation usually means a set chord progression. If we play a tune, like "Misty", the chords are an integral part of the tune. All musicians will rely on those chords, and will improvise their melodies accordingly. It is also possible to construct a type of improvisation where the chords would change according to the whims of the melody, but, in most cases, especially when more than one musician is playing, the improv feeds off the chord changes.

That is why Question & Answer is so important to this study, because it makes you think along the "mental tracks" of a jazz musician. Of course, you must start simply, using, perhaps, children's melodies or simple Mozart-like melodies. The idea is to keep your melodies *musical, simple* and *logical*. Melodies have tension and release. It is the precise handling of this tension and release that creates a good melody.

Let's Begin!

Here are some chord patterns. **(See Example 2-1, Page 70 & 71)** First start playing the *left hand chord patterns* straight across, playing the Question and then the Answer. Play one of these question and answer chord patterns until you are thoroughly in command of it. In learning in this manner, it is important to keep at it until the pattern simply *flows* from the subconscious. Then move on to the next step.

Start creating simple and logical melodies over the chord pattern. Listen to the tension and release created by the chord pattern. The I Chord has a "static" feel and the V chord has a "restless" feel. Your melody should reflect the *tensions* of the chord changes. Play the chord patterns over and over, each time seeking for new melodic patterns and fresh ideas. This will be the toughest part, because, you as a classical musician will have trouble dealing with the *simplicity* of the ideas that will be coming. You will possibly be frustrated, thinking that the ideas should be more profound and more varied. However, the advice that I give to my private students is to not be judgmental. The main idea in this exercise is to develop familiarity with playing over chord changes and to come to terms with the difficulty of creating many simple melodies. If you play on and on, the subconscious will eventually become comfortable with this activity. Remember, the study of improvisation is a mental game. We have to make changes in our subconscious mind so that we can freely *speak* the language of music.

Then, after you are totally comfortable

using the chord progressions as given, you can mix and match any chord pattern question with any chord pattern answer. For instance, you might play Question #1 and Answer #4. Notice how this completely changes your melody. The examples are given in 4/4, but any time signature can be substituted. For now, it is probably better to stick with 4/4 and 3/4. Later, try 2/4, 6/8, 5/4, 7/4, etc. Also, any accompaniment pattern can be substituted. **(See Example 2-2, Page 72 & 73)** The idea is to play one pattern over and over, continually trying to come up with new ideas. Try to keep the accompaniment patterns simple so that your main attention can be given to the melody.

Usually melodies will come out of the Major Scale of the key you are playing, but you can explore other notes. Don't use too many rules. Be musical, let your ear and innate musicianship guide you toward these melodies. If you get stuck in the middle of a melody, or if the melody does not come out right, that's OK. If that happens, perhaps you can break the rhythm at that point, and slow down or even stop. *Then compose a melody which works.* If you solve enough melodic problems, pretty soon you will begin pre-hearing these solutions before they derail you.

Try the idea of *repeating* the first two bars of the question in the first two bars of the answer. *Be logical and simple.* You want your ideas to come out at a proper resolution point. Begin soon to stretch out your ideas over a two octave range and more. The main emphasis is to not panic, and do not become frustrated if your ideas bore you. Remember, this is a simple exercise. You will probably not play the world's most profound melodies. The main point is to keep on doing it. *The subconscious mind needs to experience that act of improvising.* You will grow, but only if you continue on. Also, it is recommended *not to improvise in front of anyone else* at this point (except your piano teacher).

Later on, after your confidence increases, it will be recommended to play before and with others. It is important to have communication with other musicians and feedback from the audience.

Helpful Hints . . .

1)   Usually, when a student begins improvising on one of the patterns over and over, he has the tendency to repeat the *melodic rhythm* habitually. The melodic rhythm is the rhythm that the melody makes. (You can hear this if you clap a melody.) Then the melodies quickly become boring. Therefore, *change your melodic rhythms often*. You can even practice playing the left hand chord patterns and tapping out different melodic rhythms on your knee. Then make up melodies to match the rhythms. (Note: Kneepads are recommended for this exercise.)

2)   Also, it is a good idea to *expand your range of notes*. For instance, if you begin by choosing notes for your melody from a one-octave range, that is good but will quickly become boring. Therefore enlarge the range to two octaves or more and you will have new ideas.

3)   *Sing* along with your melody. It's amazing how this helps your sense of melodic construction.

4)   Repeat the first two bars of the melody in the first two bars of the answer. It is very important to listen to the patterns that your melodies are creating. By listening, you will think of many new ideas which will feed off of prior ideas. Of course, listen to the pitches of the melody, but also the melodic rhythm, the dynamics, the phrasing, meter and rhythm.

5.   Remember, creating a good melody is like creating a good sentence. The melody will usually end on an upswing with the V chord in the Question and settle into the I chord in the Answer.

4)   Use all your musical skills to help add interest, such as: dynamics, slurs, touches, phrasing, rubato, etc.

5)   Double or half the time value of the patterns. Use triplets. Use all manner of rhythm.

6)   Of course, *play in all keys, with different time signatures, and vary your accompaniment patterns.*

7)   Specifically vary melodic intervals. If you are playing primarily chord tones, then try scale tones. If you are playing without skips, you might specifically try large skips. Try changing registers from middle, to high, to low.

8)   Change the form of the patterns from Question and Answer to, let's say, "A B A" form.

In short anything goes, except for changing the chord pattern. Once chosen, stick with it. Once the patterns using I and V are mastered, then move on to minor (using the same V7). Then begin experimenting with I IV V I patterns. It is easy to expand into other chord progressions from this beginning exercise. The course of events is that you start with easy I V I progressions using simple accompaniments. Then progress by "opening up" your orchestration of these events. This can be accomplished in steps, perhaps by elaborating on your accompaniment patterns, such as using a Chopin Waltz accompaniment and eventually to not using any set accompaniment pattern at all, but using both hands to provide the motion. This is explained further in the section on modal improvisation.

EXAMPLE 2-1 - QUESTION AND ANSWER

EXAMPLE 2-2 QUESTION AND ANSWER - SAMPLE ACCOMPANIMENTS

Major

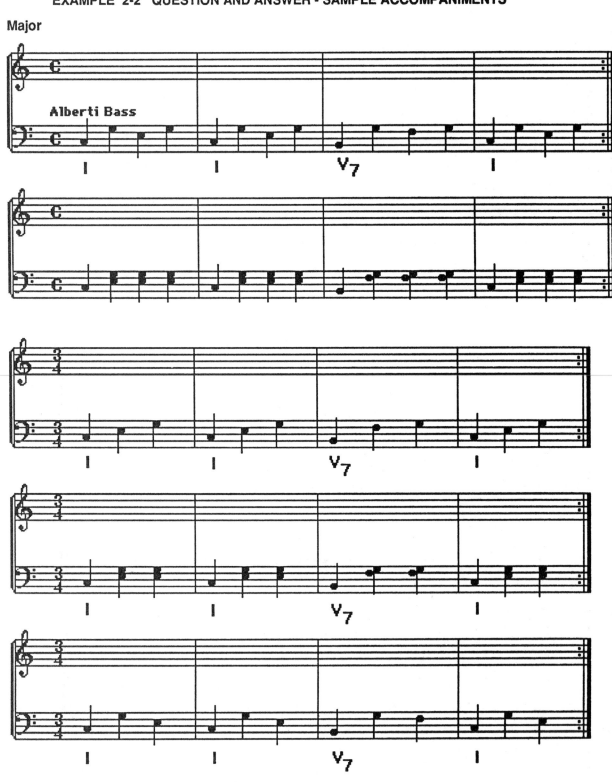

Minor

20. THIRDS AND SIXTHS

You can also expand the "orchestration". Try playing the melodies in thirds and sixths. A good way to start using thirds and sixths is to take simple melodies such as "Three Blind Mice" and play in thirds and sixths. Put the melody on top and add the third or sixth lower than the melody.   Let the *ear* tell you whether or not to use either a third or a sixth. Sometimes they are interchangable, but often harmonic or melodic implications will force you to make a choice. Soon you should be an expert in "pre-hearing" these thirds and sixths. Then play your Q & A melodies first in single notes, *then repeat in thirds and sixths.* When you do this, for simplicity, try using only a single bass note in the left hand. **(See Example 2-3)**

After this becomes easy for you to do (in all keys), then we can blend this exercise with the open voicings exercise. (Please refer to the Open Voicings Exercises later in this chapter.)

EXAMPLE 2-3   THIRDS AND SIXTHS

21. MAJOR SCALE IMPROVISATION

One of the first improvisation exercises that we can practice is simply improvising using a Major Scale. This is kind of like playing with silly putty or fingerpainting with sound. The fun part of playing with fingerpainting is that we do not need any lessons or rules to paint our paintings. We simply experiment, and thus have fun. If we use the Major Scale to improvise, we can use any of the notes, in any order, with any rhythm, in any density and in any style. We have no rules about which hand plays the melody or, for that matter, whether or not there is a melody. The main point is to play and to experience music. Of course, we should play this exercise in *all* Major Scales, no favoritism please.

Of course, just thinking about jumping in and improvising will send shivers up and down some student's backs. There are problems, to be sure, in learning to improvise. However, the best way to solve these problems is to first recognize that they are there. Second we should try to list them, and thirdly, do our best to *solve* them. So, before we begin improvising let's first examine some of the obstacles.

1)   We are generally not used to putting music into motion and then interrelating with the music "on the fly".

2)   Our left hand and right hand wants to take on specific functions, such as: right hand plays the melody and left hand plays a recurring accompaniment pattern. This usually bogs us down in playing the same trite patterns over and over.

3)   The left hand and right hand have not achieved independence. This is very important because if the hands always work together we are limited in the depth of our improvisational ideas.

4) We do not have a good control over melody making. This includes understanding sequences. It also includes phrasing.

5) Our piano technique limits us to what we can play. This is important, because if, internally, we think that we can not play something, because the fingers will not move fast enough, then our conscious mind will simply negate playing the idea.

6) Our fingering practices are not automatic. This is very important because, once again if we subconsciously feel that we can not successfully finger something, then we will not try to play it at all.

7) We have not made a study of specific styles of playing. This is important because most pieces that we will improvise will emulate one style or another.

8) Our rhythmic sense isn't solid. We are not used to establishing a "groove", which is a solid, emotional, rhythmic feel.

9) We are not used to playing music with a jazz technique, which ultimately would give the music an overall jazz sound.

This book intends to offer solutions to these problems by offering specific advice on improvisation, discussing solutions to technical problems and presenting ideas on specific styles. In performing improvisation using the modes, the problems of what to play harmonically, are automatically solved. Therefore we can concentrate on the areas of playing in motion, hand independence, establishing rhythm, technical solutions, and stylistic directions.

Playing in Motion

This is an area that we perhaps do not think about when we are playing our classical pieces. Music, by its very nature, is in motion. It is constantly on the move. However, this is an issue which reaches supreme importance while improvising because it takes a certain type of thinking. Jazz musicians get a lot of practice in this area by performing in clubs and playing with other musicians. Certainly, the pressure is on, when you sit in a jam session and have to perform well.

The best way to develop confidence in this area is to practice "in motion". The more you try, the more your subconscious will develop familiarity with this skill and subsequently, the more you will develop confidence. If you have an opportunity to practice with a group, another musician, as an accompanist, as a church organist, etc., this will greatly help you to achieve this goal.

The following exercise is called the Motion Exercise and is designed to give you practice in these areas. As said many times, please do not get frustrated, and please keep trying! There will be many plateaus and many breakthroughs . . . just keep trying.

Motion Exercise

1) Alternating arms - just start playing a rhythmic pattern with your hands, on your lap. I have talked to many students who have insisted that they do not have good rhythm and have found that they have never isolated pure rhythm as a study. For instance, if you are playing a piece of music, rhythm is mixed in with melody and harmony. Very often this creates confusion

and, as a result, the rhythm is the first thing which breaks down. Rhythm is a subliminal activity in the music in that, even though it is notated in the music, the actual rhythmic activity is supplied by the performer. Therefore it is important that the performer develop good rhythm independently of melody and harmony.

Very often, the same student who states that he does not have good rhythm, is super on the dance floor and is easily capable of following the rhythm chant at a football game. Drummers are usually the best at rhythm because they give rhythm their full attention.

Actually, all I am suggesting is that you start by clapping out a recurring beat pattern while alternating the hands (arms). Keep it going, see if you can really become familiar with the beat pattern.

Now transfer this beat pattern to the keyboard by playing some clusters from the Major Scale. Don't worry if the clusters make sense. We have to start somewhere. One idea is to play a single bass note in the left hand and alternate with a chord in the right hand. Try changing registers on the keyboard and try using different densities of textures. The main point is to keep the rhythmic pattern that you have established. Here are a few examples of rhythmic patterns. You can use them or not, and certainly make up your own. **(See Example 2-4)**

.You should practice this often until you develop familiarity with the beat pattern, rhythm, and the sounds of the Major Scale. Definitely change keys, time signatures, phrasing or articulation. Just have fun, and do not expect too much at this point. The reason that you are doing this is to establish the feeling of playing rhythm with your arms. The notes are not too important at this point.

EXAMPLE 2-4 ALTERNATING RIGHT AND LEFT HAND BEATS

2)   Alternating within one hand - This exercise is very similar to the first except that you are alternating your rhythmic pattern within one hand, usually between the thumb and the other fingers, and also alternating with the other hand. Often the left hand will play a single bass note while the right hand alternates between the thumb and other fingers.

3)   Continuous stream of notes - In this exercise you will start a continuous stream of eighth notes, carefully choosing your notes so that they resolve at appropriate places. Let your ear tell you where the appropriate places are. At first you will have to go very slow, but as your skill increases, you can pick up steam. Keep your rhythmic pattern going throughout the exercise. Next try eighth note triplets, then sixteenth notes. Finally play a combination of quarter notes, eighth notes, eighth note triplets and sixteenth notes. At this point it is

suggested that you beat out patterns varying between the time values without playing notes, then when you are comfortable, play with notes. For simplicity, the left hand can play a single bass note.

4. Combination Exercise - now start combining all the exercises. Be sure to keep the rhythm going and try all manner of combinations of alternating between and within the hands, and using continuous single notes.

I want to emphasize that you not be too critical of your improvisations, at this point. The idea is to get used to being in continuous movement, thinking on your feet, so to speak. Once you have developed confidence in this area, many doors toward improvisation will open to you.

22. THE MAJOR SCALE MODES

The Modes are really very simple to understand. *Take any scale and begin the scale on a degree of that scale other than 1 - 1.* In the case of the Major Scale, 1 - 1 also has a modal name, that of *Ionian Mode.* If we start on the second degree and move from 2 - 2, we are playing the *Dorian Mode,* 3 - 3 is the *Phrygian,* 4 - 4 is the *Lydian,* 5 - 5 is the *Mixolydian,* 6 - 6 is the *Aeolian,* and 7 - 7 is the *Locrian.* In the scale of C Major, C - C is 1 - 1, D - D is 2 - 2, etc. Take a few minutes and *memorize* the numbers and names of the modes, right now! **(See Examples 2-5 and 2-6)**

EXAMPLE 2-5   MODES AND THEIR CHARACTERISTICS

Degrees of the Scale	Modal Name	Characteristics
1 - 1	IONIAN	(Same as Major Scale.)
2 - 2	DORIAN	Flat 3 and 7 (Sounds Minor)
3 - 3	PHRYGIAN	Flat 2, 3, 6, 7 (Sounds Minor with Flatted 2nd)
4 - 4	LYDIAN	Sharp 4 (Sounds Major with Sharped 4th)
5 - 5	MIXOLYDIAN	Flat 7 (Works well with Dominant 7th)
6 - 6	AEOLIAN	Flat 3, 6, & 7 (Same as Relative Minor Scale)
7 - 7	LOCRIAN	Flat 2, 3, 5, 6, 7 (Works well with Half Diminished)

Now you would possibly think that all these modes would sound like the parent Major Scale since all the modes have the same *notes* as the Major. However, this is *not* the case. In fact, this is why I have not included the parent scale in the analysis. Each mode has its own "mood" or personality due to the different positions of the half steps to whole steps. As you remember, the Major Scale has a special feeling due to the half steps between 3 & 4 and 7 & 8. The Dorian Mode, for example, sounds completely different due to the half steps shifting to 2 & 3 and 6 & 7. This mode sounds minor-ish due to the minor third.

Modal Exercise

It is recommended that each mode be learned separately as its own scale. Each one retains its own emotional feeling and will be used by the improviser for a specific purpose. The following is a method to learn the modes individually.

Begin by choosing a bottom note. That note will be the foundation note throughout the exercise. First improvise freely using the C Major Scale using the same instructions for the Motion Exercise. Then after the C Major scale is thoroughly experienced, then sharp the 4th degree and you will be improvising on the Lydian. You could say in your mind that you are really playing a G Major Scale, but this is *not* recommended. As said before, it is better to experience the mode as your listener experiences it, as its own scale. Then, continue on through the modes by adding only one changed note at a time. **(See Example 2-6, Page 86)**

Next play the Mixolydian, which has a flatted seventh. Then add a flatted 3rd to the flatted 7th to play the Dorian. Now add the flat 6th to the flat 3rd and flat 7th to form the Aeolian Mode. Then add the flatted

2nd for the Phrygian and then the flatted 5th for the Locrian. Each time you are changing the scale by just one note. **(See Example 2-6 & 2-7, Pages 86 & 87)**

Ideas for Modal Playing

1)   Modes have a tendency not to lead anywhere. When playing the mode, it is similar to finger-painting, just revel in the fun of making different combinations of sounds. Try different textures.

2)   Do not think of chords, think of textures. Actually, "chords" are really two or more notes played at the same time. In modes, we are choosing notes from a series of notes. Try to pre-hear this series of notes and then choose two or more to play at the same time. Try to avoid naming them as specific chords or inversions of chords. The idea is to just hear the sounds that they make.

3)   Do not allow the hands to assume specific musical functions. The most common example is to have the left hand play chords or accompaniment figures while the right hand exclusively plays the melody. Try to look down on the keyboard and "see" what you want to play, regardless of which hand plays. This is similar to an orchestrator who is writing for instruments other than the piano. He is "hearing" the sounds in his head, the position of the hands on the keyboard is not important.

4)   Have fun with rhythms. Try new rhythmic patterns. Also enjoy getting into a "groove" by playing these patterns over and over. Experiment with different tempi and rubato. Try 3 against 2 and other polyrhythms. Also you can derive rhythmic impetus from any note in either hand. This is important, so that you don't always look to the left hand for rhythmic movement. The movement, for example, can come from both hands

fingering a broken chord.

5)   Always play musically. Use dynamics, phrasing, touches, good timing and good tone.

6)   A good idea is to have a specific start to your improvisation. Then, by applying concentration, follow your idea to a final conclusion. Try to avoid endless playing. Keep asking yourself for descriptive words of what you are playing. You might describe your current improv as "mysterious", "loving", "bombastic", "tender", "searching", etc. By putting a label on it you have an idea where you are going and where you have been.

7)   <u>Don't over-pedal</u>. When you over-pedal, you trivialize the melodies that you are creating because they are not clear and well-defined.

8)   Think conceptually. Modal has too many notes which "work". You must limit parameters and concepts. Think of movie scoring. Think of telling a story or describing a painting.

9)   Try four note phrases. Then string two four-note phrases together.

10)   More ideas for modal improv: colors, shapes, textures, accompaniments, and ostinato.

After you have developed the ability to play modal improvisation on each of the modes, in all keys, you can try other ideas.

Other Ideas

1)   Play C Dorian for awhile and alternate with another Dorian, perhaps F Dorian. Or you can continue on to another Dorian. Of course, you can play

with any of the modes in this manner or mix the modes if you wish. You can start with any key. What you are doing here, is similar to what you will be doing when you play through chord changes. Chords really are notes from a scale or a mode. The word "Tonality" can describe any series of notes, either scale or mode. If you have been given the chords in a piece of music, then each chord can be translated into the tonality from which it is a part. Then, you can play from tonality to tonality through the piece. This is the basis for improvisation in jazz. So, practice playing modal improvisations so that it will be easy and natural for you to improvise over the chord changes of a tune.

2)   Try playing to records which are designed for music study, such as *Jamey Aebersold's Jazz Improvisation Series*. The first record, for example, has some modal improvisations on it.

EXAMPLE 2-6` MAJOR SCALE MODES EXERCISE

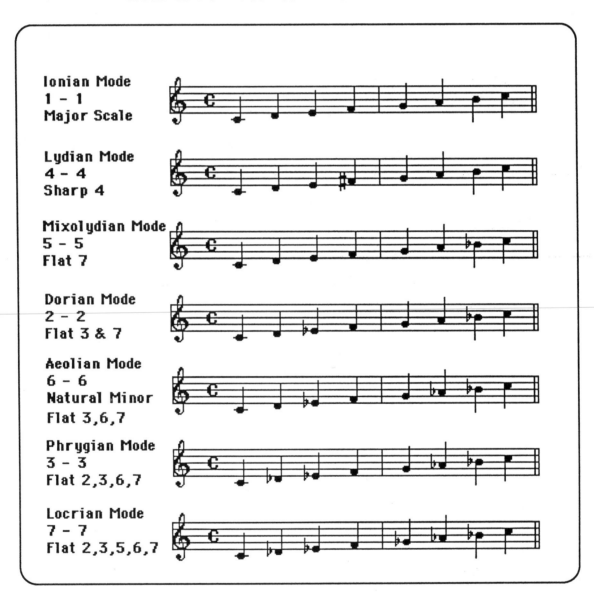

EXAMPLE 2-7 MODAL EXERCISE - STEP BY STEP

Begin by choosing a bottom note. That note will be the foundation note throughout the exercise. In this example, we will start by improvising freely using the C Major Scale. Then C will continue as our "bottom note".

**Ionian Mode
1 – 1
Major Scale**

C is the bottom note for each example.

Then after the C Major scale is thoroughly experienced, then sharp the 4th degree and you will be improvising on the Lydian. You could say in your mind that you are really playing a G Major Scale, but this is *not* recommended. As said before, it is better to experience the mode as your listener experiences it, as its own scale.

**Lydian Mode
4 – 4
Sharp 4**

Then, continue on through the modes by adding only one changed note at a time. Next play the Mixolydian, which has a flatted seventh.

**Mixolydian Mode
5 – 5
Flat 7**

Then add a flatted 3rd to the flatted 7th to play the Dorian.

**Dorian Mode
2 – 2
Flat 3 & 7**

Now add the flat 6th to the flat 3rd and flat 7th to form the Aeolian Mode.

Aeolian Mode
6 – 6
Natural Minor
Flat 3,6,7

Then add the flatted 2nd for the Phrygian.

Phrygian Mode
3 – 3
Flat 2,3,6,7

And finally, the flatted 5th for the Locrian. Each time you are changing the scale by just one note.

Locrian Mode
7 – 7
Flat 2,3,5,6,7

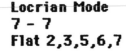

23. OPEN VOICING EXERCISE

Now we are going to use the Advanced Open Voicings that we learn in the Foundations chapter. **(Chapter 1, Section 15 & 16, Pages 46 - 52)** You will remember that you practiced I - IV - I, I - V - I, and I - IV - V - I progressions. It is recommended that you endeavor to put these progressions in a musical manner. You can use I, IV, & V in any order. Let the melody suggest the harmony. . This should be especially easy for church organists and pianists, since they have ample opportunity to improvise during services. Once you have perfected moving in a musical fashion using the I, IV, and V chords, then start adding in other chords into the mix. The next chord to add in would probably be the sixth, which in its natural state in the Major Scale is a minor or minor seventh. **(See Example 2-8)**

EXAMPLE 2-8 OPEN VOICINGS PROGRESSION I - VI - IV - V - I

24. PACHELBEL'S CANON EXERCISE

Pachelbel's Canon can be used as a basis for improvisation. Even though the composition was originally written in D, I am writing the example in C for simplicity's sake. Of course, you are invited to learn it in *all keys*. This is fun to play, and you should have good results very soon. **(See Example 2-10)**

a) Learn the melody, bass note, and chord progression. Memorize the numbers of the chord progression: ie. I,V,VI,III,IV,I,IV,V. (See #1)

b) Play many open voicings on each chord.

c) Improvise through the chord progression using open voicings.

d) Play melodies from the top voice while holding the open voicing. **(Example 2-10, #4 , Page 92)**

e) Play melodies from the second from the top voice while holding the open voicing.

f) Play melodies from the third from the top voice while holding the open voicing.

g) Play melodies from the bottom voice while holding the open voicing.

h) Now practice moving the interval of a tenth in parallel motion. You can also move thirds and sixths.

EXAMPLE 2-10 PACHELBEL CANON EXERCISE

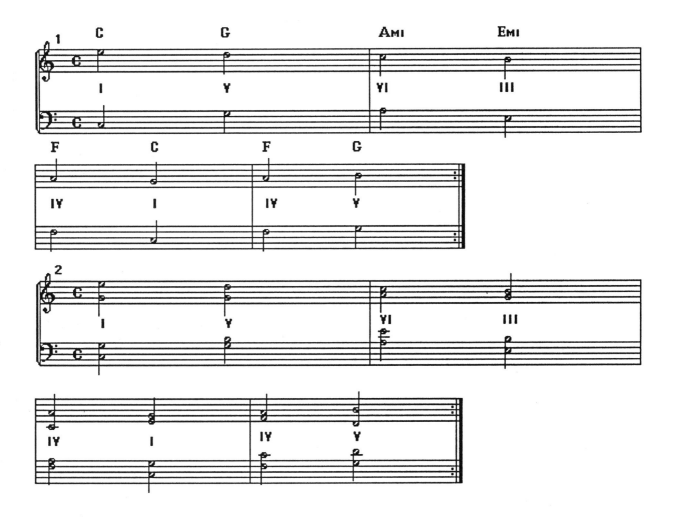

Beginning Improvisation Review

QUESTION AND ANSWER

1)   Have you been playing lots and lots of *Question and Answer*? Don't forget, the challenge is to play one pattern over and over, constantly coming up with new melodies. Then, try a new pattern, and perhaps change the rhythm or meter. Try new keys, etc. Challenge yourself to come up with new melodies. Also, try, for awhile to play a *constant* eighth note, eighth note triplet or sixteenth note solo. Then, add in space and phrasing. You should practice this until you are comfortable with soloing over the chord changes. **(Example 2-1, Pages 70 & 71)**

Completed: Date_____

2)   Play *Question and Answer* in Minor. Experiment using different *minor* scales (Melodic, Harmonic and Natural) and minor-sounding modes (Dorian, Phrygian, and Aeolian) for soloing. If these scales and modes are new to you, they will be presented in future chapters.) **(Example 2-1, Page 71)**

Completed: Date_____

3)   Did you try the *Sample Accompaniments* for Question and Answer? Did you try to make up your own accompaniment patterns? In Major? Im Minor? **(Example 2-2, Pages 72 & 73)**

Completed: Date_____

4)   Experiment with playing familiar melodies in *Thirds and Sixths*. Also play Question and Answer in thirds and sixths. **(Example 2-3, Page 74)**

Completed: Date_____

MAJOR SCALE IMPROVISATION

5)   Practice the *Motion Exercise*. This will take alot of practice until you are completely comfortable with improvising while in motion. If you have a problem with rhythm, then pat on your knee until you are familiar with rhythm, itself. Then transfer your rhythmic sense to the improv. Don't give up on this one. You *will* improve over time. Put a special emphasis on the "continuous stream of notes" exercise. This exercise helps "hook you up" from your brain to your hands. **(Example 2-4, Pages 77 - 80)**

Completed: Date_____

4)   Have you memorized the *Major Scale Modes.* **(Example 2-5, Page 81)**   This may take awhile.

Completed: Date_____

5)   Have you practiced the *Modal Exercise*? This exercise is an extension on the Major Scale Improv and is extremely important! You are encouraged to keep trying to come up with new improvisations and new experimentations. Practice this until you feel totally confident that you have the ability to come up with musical ideas each time you begin playing. Don't forget to experiment with different rhythms. **(Example 2-6, Page 86) (Example 2-7, Pages 87& 88)**

Completed: Date_____

OPEN VOICINGS

6)   Can you play the *Open Voicings Exercise* using I, IV, V, I in any order, and create entire improvisations. First think of the melody, then harmonize the melody. Perhaps it would help to think of a church organ improvisation. Definitely, try this in all keys until you can flow on and on. **(Refer to Chapter One, Sections 14 - 16, Pages 46 - 52)** You can also add in other chords such as the VI chord **(Example 2-8, Page 89)** You have to be able to control this type of improvisation and the only way to learn is to . . . practice.

Completed: Date_____

PACHELBEL'S CANON EXERCISE

8)   Are you very familiar improvising on the chord changes of *"Pachelbel's Canon"*. Play this improv in all keys. See how many different melodic ideas you can create. This gives you a very musical way to handle the open voicings. Play all the steps of this exercise. **(Page 90)**. This exercise should be practiced until you can play on an on, without changing the chords or stumbling on the melodic flow. **(Example 2-10, Pages 91 & 92)**

Completed: Date_____

Note: This Chapter presents a way to start improvising. If you try the exercises and give up quickly, you will not develop the skills necessary to become a good improviser. Even if you feel that you are "not getting it", it is my hope that you will persevere. It takes a little time for the subconscious to become used to the activity of improvising and the musical theory. Many of my students have had breakthroughs, where, after a long period of frustrations, began to easily improvise. Keep trying!

3 Technique for Improvisation

Many classical pianists, I believe, feel that *classical* piano technique is the best technique for *all* kinds of piano music. This is understandable considering that classical technique is the piano technique that they have been taught. There are also many who feel that jazz technique is just sloppy, incorrect technique and that it should be avoided at all costs. There is also the feeling that you can not *learn* to play jazz with a good "feel" and that the good players are born with their style and sound.

In my opinion, a technique is simply a method of doing something which helps you to achieve a desired end. Therefore, if it is effective, it is good. Secondly, I don't believe that the standard classical technique will always work in other musical areas and that there has to be some variation to give you the required stylings. Thirdly, there are many different eras and developments in the classical repertoire which require specialized techniques and specific interpretation to play correctly. This is true in the pop and jazz fields also. The technique used to play a funky blues would be completely different from, a **Bill Evans** jazz style, and different again from a **George Winston** improvisation. It is important to match the technique to the style.

I do believe that there are some technical traits which can be discussed and learned which will give the classical pianist a good jazz sound, but the classical pianist must give up some possible longstanding biases about good technique and be willing to try some new, and perhaps radical approaches to achieve certain jazz styles. Also, it will take some practice to develop these different techniques. And you will have to spend many hours listening to and studying jazz and pop pianists to develop their sound.

It is recommended that you expand your listening to hear pianists that you do not normally listen to. Buy or borrow records or record tapes that can be listened to in your car. Listen critically and try to discover how the pianist achieves the sound. Listen for phrasing and dynamics. Listen for pedaling. In short, listen as critically to the jazz pianist as you would a classical pianist performing, let's say, Debussy. Try sitting at the piano, and play while the pianist is playing. It doesn't matter if you are playing the right notes, just try for the right touch and phrasing. Try to put yourself in the pianist's shoes. See youself doing what he does.

I believe that there is a common misconception in many jazz methods that you can explain the jazz sound or groove by saying that it is a "rolling three" feel with the notes played on the first and third of the three. I feel that if you listen to different jazz players, you will discover that this is greatly oversimplified and in many cases, simply untrue. The best way to develop a style is to *listen to specific phrases*, then play those recorded phrases over and over, trying to *sing* them. Then transfer that phrase, as well as you can, to the piano trying to copy your singing. Phrasing is the answer to learning jazz styles. Sometimes you can find written jazz solos by, let's say, Oscar Peterson or Bill Evans. You can find the original recording and then listen, phrase by phrase and try to copy his touch. It is as complicated as trying to imitate or learn a specific dialect within a language. Actually, this is an area in which a classical player should be at home, since he spends much of his time trying to play classical pieces in their "correct" interpretation.

It is interesting, though, that the way that most classical methods teach technique do not help the pianist to become an improviser. A great deal of emphasis is often given to playing scales and arpeggios always in the same way, usually from bottom to top, with the same tempo, the same dynamic level, the same rhythm and the same touch. Arpeggios are usually played in the root position. Hanon, for instance is often only played in the original key of "C" and in the original rhythmic patterns. In other words, there isn't much emphasis on creating variety. Also there isn't much room for spontaneity. This often leads to boredom and results in mechanical playing.

I feel that ultimately the way that you practice your technique will result in your "style". In other words, the subconscious mind will learn these subtleties, and then they will become part of the involuntary actions of the subconscious. Once this happens, then when you play a composition or perform an improvisation, this becomes your general way of playing. It becomes your musical "personality". I recommend practicing your technique in a similar manner to the way you want to eventually perform.

25. GENERAL TECHNIQUES FOR IMPROVISATION

1) Variable Speed

When playing a scale, arpeggio or Hanon, try playing as if you were playing with a *variable speed dial*. Smoothly turn the tempo up and down, move from very slow to very fast. This helps to de-emphasize the rigidity of the exercise and to develop a natural control. This is helpful in playing rubato. It is also very helpful in the development of the improviser as it gives a greater range of expression from which to draw.

Evenness in music is not exact evenness. If it was, then computers could "quantize" music into perfection. Quantizing is when a computer shifts all notes to a specific note value, such as to the sixteenth note. In this matter the music is perfectly even, but not very musical. In one computer music program, they even have a command called "humanize" to develop the correct amount of imperfection.

Therefore, it would seem that perfect evenness is not the correct goal, but, rather, *control*. This control can be developed by practicing variable speed.

2) Variable Dynamics

In the same manner, it is recommended that you practice in variable dynamics, from soft to loud, in all manner. This can be done while practicing scales and arpeggios.

3) Root, third, fifth arpeggios

Choose a bottom root note, let's say "C". "C" is the root of C Major Triad. It is also the major 3rd of "A flat Major Triad, and the fifth of "F Major Triad". **(See Example 3-1)**

When playing as an arpeggio, *randomly* select which triad you will be playing as you move up and down. **(See Example 3-2)** Note the fingerings given for right hand and left hand fingerings. In general, if playing two handed arpeggios, try to have the thumb play at the same time with both hands. Also, if starting on a black note, put the thumb on the first available white key. Of course, try not to put the thumb on a black key. When playing a F Sharp or G Flat Major arpeggio, any order of fingering goes. After learning the major triads, learn the

EXAMPLE 3-1   ROOT, THIRD, FIFTH TRIADS

Root   3rd   5th

EXAMPLE 3-2   ROOT, THIRD, FIFTH ARPEGGIOS

minor, augmented and diminished triads.

4) Random Arpeggios

Now play the Major Arpeggios in a totally random manner, moving at will from chord to chord. You may change directions, up and down, at any time and can even change in the middle of a chord. Also feel free to start arpeggios in inversions other than the root. You can move from one major triad arpeggio either directly, by diatonic (scale), or chromatic movement. Playing with two hands is recommended. Try to let the thumbs play at the same time.

Try playing in different rhythmical patterns, in different dynamics, touches and phrases. You can also play arpeggios, for instance, with the root in the left hand and the third in the right hand. In fact you can play arpeggios with one arpeggio in the left hand and a different arpeggio in the right hand. After learning the major triads, try the minor, augmented and diminished triads. In other words, experiment, experiment, experiment!

5) Random Scales

You can also play scales in a randomized manner. For instance, you can practice Major Scales by moving up the scale, let's say, in C Major and then arbitrarily moving to E Major and then again moving up or down using B Flat Major. This is fun to do, especially when you are playing with two hands. Of course, keeping track of *fingering* is the main problem to solve.

Fingering is an act of the subconcious mind when improvising. By practicing exercises which stress random movement, the subconsious learns how to think ahead so the the *fingering is automatic*. This skill is very important because we will tend to organize our musical ideas according to our ability to finger them. In other words, if we know, subconsciously that we can not successfully finger a passage, we will quickly choose not to play it. Therefore, in practicing using two hands playing an octave or two apart, we are training this function of fingering in the subconscious thereby opening up more ideas for us to play. Start very slow and pick up speed as the fingering flows more easily.

As with the arpeggios, experiment with different rhythms, etc. The more you try new ideas and keep playing, the quicker you will develop into a fine improviser.

It should go without saying that you should always play as musically as possible, with special emphasis on playing with good tone, legato and phrasing. The scales and arpeggios can be freely mixed in any manner.

6) Seventh Chord Arpeggios

Take any seventh chord and play it up and down in a beautiful arpeggio. Take care not to meter beat, which means to let the arm swing with the chord. Be particularly careful to evenly play one note to the next with each note getting its full value and also even weight. Practice legato and staccato, in rhythms etc. Also you can develop randomness by switching "mid-stream" to different seventh chords, not always in their root positions. These should also be played with both hands. You can mix with Scales and Triad Arpeggios.

The emphasis is to *keep moving.* In this way you will develop good fingering habits in regards to improvisation. Also you are priming the subconscious to "think on your feet" because you are in constant movement and are playing according to your spontaneous whims. You can also play in different time values, such as eighth notes, eighth note triplets and sixteenth notes. You don't have to play fast, at first. Let your mind get used to this kind of thinking and movement.

26. LEGATO PLAYING AND PHRASING

I would like to say a few words about legato playing and phrasing. In jazz, as it is in classical, legato playing should be the most basic element of piano technique. It is emphasized because it is not natural to play legato on the piano. The piano is basically a *percussion* instrument with hammers that strike strings and banging on the piano is perhaps the most natural way to play. Therefore special emphasis must be placed on simply moving from one note to another in a smooth fashion. I know that most of you have spent many hours working on your perfect legato and glorious tone, but for the benefit of others, I would like to quickly share some ideas on good tone, legato and phrasing. Believe me, this will apply directly to the next chapter which is on Jazz Improvisation.

The piano responds directly to weight. It is good to have as much control over weight as possible to utilize its full range of potential. In this regard, I often start beginning students exploring the full dynamic range of the piano by learning how to play loud without banging. This is accomplished by relaxation, speed, and correct use of body weight. The following exercise will demonstrate how to use the natural body weight.

1)   Move the piano bench back. To know how far back, sit off the front third of the bench and place the right foot on the right pedal (damper pedal). The body should be a comfortable distance from the piano.

2)   Sit upright with good posture. Lean slightly forward and let your arms hang loosely from the shoulders. Allow the hands to rest on the piano with full dead body weight. I know that sounds awful but the arms should feel totally dead-weight. The hands should be simply resting on the keyboard, on the bottom of the keybed.

3)   Now shift the dead-weight to the finger tips. To do this relax the elbow. Make sure that the hand and wrist do not collapse. Also don't let the first joint in the finger collapse. The hand and finger must be strong, and the wrist strong, but springy.

4) Put the arm weight over the thumb in the right hand and move the weight from the thumb to the fifth finger. You can play C to G, for instance. A good analogy is to stand on your feet with the feet slightly apart. Move the body weight back and forth smoothly between the feet and feel the weight moving back and forth. Now do this with your fingers and you can feel the weight on one side of the hand and feel it move smoothly to the other side of the hand.

5) Play the C, then play the G by shifting the weight. Let them both ring at the same time with the weight equally over both of them. Then shift the weight to the G and release, just lift the C. This should clear the blur and only the G is playing. Then shift back to the C, let both play, then shift the weight all to the C and release the G.

6) Now this exercise can be played with arpeggios. Play the C with the weight over the C; move to the E, with both the C and E playing; move the weight to the E and release the C. Do this throughout the arpeggio.

7) To develop a beautiful legato simply shorten the time of the blur. If you want a totally clean legato, change the weight simultaneously. If you want a lush legato, have a *little* blur between the notes. (Not enough that anyone would hear it.)

8) Play this exercise using all arpeggios, scales, Hanon, whatever to develop a beautiful, weighted legato tone. The arms, especially the elbows, must be relaxed allowing the fingers to rest on the keybed, not on the top of the keyboard. Do not cave in the fingers, hands, or wrists. Keep the weight forward into the keys.

9)   Make up melodies, using both hands play the same notes one or two octaves apart. You can start by simply playing intervals. Play them as legato and with as much feeling as possible.

27. THE PIANO AS A GONG

This is an exercise in playing and hearing the fullest expanse of the keyboard. I usually assign this exercise to a beginning student to have them explore the loud dynamic limits of the piano and to know that they can achieve loudness without bad tone. Many students play fearfully, with tension because they haven't had this experience. They should feel their energy flow in and with the piano and not feel separate from it.

The exercise simply is to play a full triad in both hands over and over, in a steady rhythm. The triad can be played up and down the keyboard. The student is encouraged to think of a concerto. The beat should be about 60 beats per minute. The idea is to develop a continual wave action in the arms with the striking point at the tips of the fingers. The action is similar to snapping a bull whip. The main emphasis is that the arms be dead-weight and totally relaxed.

If the piano is played over and over with the *damper pedal held down*, the result is similar to repeatedly striking a gong. The gong picks up more and more vibrations as you strike it until it has reached a total vibration. Once the piano has reached that point, the student can experience the complete fullness of the piano. Now the student can measure between very soft and very loud and should have a better musical command over dynamics.

28. ROTATION EXERCISE

This exercise was first given to me as a young student by **Frederic Saatman**. It explains a basic wrist rotation technique which is excellent in developing good phrasing and legato. I am not suggesting that this technique is proper for all types of piano playing or musical styles, however it is especially invaluable in playing jazz or any style which requires weighted phrasing. This technique is appropriate for Romantic, Impressionistic, and Contemporary compositions but less appropriate for Baroque and Classical Period compositions. Also it works well for many pop styles and jazz styles, but not all.

Another point is that this method requires relaxation, and as such is very helpful in increasing speed on the keyboard. It also lends itself to any kind of textural playing, such as some Debussy pieces and many "New Age" improvisational pieces.

1) Place five fingers of each hand over the whole tone scale. The thumb of the right hand is over the middle "E" and the thumb of the left hand is over the middle "C". The fingers fan in opposite directions over the whole tone scale from that point.

2) The wrists are slightly high. To get the correct position, it is suggested that you place your fingers over the whole tone scale with the thumbs on "C" and "E" and then *move the wrists in* until they are either touching or almost touching. The fingers at this point are fanning outward. This gives us the capability of rocking from the inside to the outside.

3) Play the thumbs on "C" and "E" and rock back and forth between the thumbs and second fingers. The second finger on the left hand will play a "B Flat" and

the second finger on the right hand will play an "F Sharp". Rock back and forth using the wrists to move the hand. The action feels like the spokes on a wagon wheel being moved back and forth.

4)   Now rock back and forth between adjacent fingers, 2 - 3; 3 - 4; 4 - 5; 5 - 4; 4 - 3; 3 - 2; and 2 - 1. (Hands are moving in contrary motion.) Keep the fingers rather straight with a very slight curve. Again, think of spokes on a wheel. The wrists must be moving back and forth.

5)   Rock over three fingers, 1 - 2 - 3 ; 2 - 3 - 4; 3 - 4 - 5; 5 - 4 - 3; 4 - 3 - 2; and 3 - 2 - 1.

6)   Rock back and forth between four fingers, 1 - 2 - 3 - 4.

7)   Rotate over all five fingers. The fingers are guided by the wrist. The fingers are *not* lifting and falling. If you do *not* see the wrists moving back and forth, the exercise is not being done correctly.

8)   While continuously rotating over the five fingers, start accenting one finger each complete rotation. For instance, first accent the thumbs, then the second fingers, then the third fingers etc. You can begin the rotation with the accented finger.

9)   Now use this techique to rotate between random notes that you will spontaneously choose. In other words make up your own melody. Think of a cello or another melodic instrument and play with expression.

29. RECOMMENDED PIANO TECHNIQUE METHOD BOOKS

There have been many methods of piano technique that I have used through the years, but some in particular, have more meaning to the improviser. The criteria that I use for these books are as follows:

1)   The exercises should be easily playable in all keys.

2)   The exercises should operate the fingers in many patterns.

3)   The exercises should lend themselves to exploration of different harmonies, rhythms, phrasing, touches, dynamics, etc.

4)   The exercises should help develop the hand in specific ways, ie: strength, flexibility, coordination, sensitivity and control.

Some of the methods that I use and recommend are as follows:

a) Hanon - especially if practiced in all keys, in different rhythms, touches, dynamics, and with variable tempo. It is most important to have the student play the exercises as musically as possible. Of course, Hanon should be practiced with good piano tone. Hanon Revisited by Arthur Gold and Robert Fizdale is helpful in changing the patterns. Again this is improved upon by playing in all keys, rhythms etc.

b) Pischna - 60 exercises are my favorite of Pischna's exercises. This is very good for finger and hand coordination. Exercises are played in all keys.

c) Philipp - Exercises for the Independence of the Fingers - very good for building finger strength and developing ability to play large chords.

d) Robert Pace Method - This is an excellent method especially for teaching children to improvise and to play in all keys. The technical principles are designed with the improviser in mind.

d) Alfred Cortot - Principles of Pianoforte Technique - this is my current favorite. Cortot seems to have come up with just the right formula for exercises which develop improvisational abilities. There are many reasons that I particularly like this method, for example:

1) All the exercises are played in many different ways. Depending on the exercise, the student is encouraged to explore all keys, different harmonic progressions, many different rhythms and different touches, mainly legato and staccato. This adds freshness to the exercises and helps to develop many different technical abilities.

2) There is a novel idea to have daily warmup exercises for the fingers, wrists and arms. Not only do these exercises warm you up, they help to develop technical ability by increasing stretches and strength. Also these exercises are practiced in different keys, rhythms, etc.

3) There are several sections of the book, each helping to solve different technical problems.

4) Many of the patterns can be easily adapted to become jazz improvisation patterns.

The mailing addresses and publishers of these books are listed in the section entitled *Further Study.*

30. JAZZ TECHNIQUES

We can make a few generalizations about jazz technique, which have to be refined further as we get into specific styles.

1) There is a greater tendency to use arm weight. This is especially true in the heavier jazz styles, such as early blues. Phrases and parts of phrases are intensified by this arm weight. The wrists are slightly looser and the shoulder weight is brought into play.

2) Even though legato playing is the fundamental touch, as it is in classical playing, individual note *durations* are more varied. In other words, in classical, the legatos and stacattos are fairly even and regulated. By duration, I am referring to the length of time that the individual note sounds. This term is often used in regards to synthesizer playing and in computerized sequencing.

In jazz, you often clip off the *end* of the duration and leave a slight space. If you listen to big band music and then try to exactly sing the phrases, you can experience what I mean. One of the things which gives jazz a completely different sound from classical is this variation of note durations. This duration changes from phrases and from style to style. In general the sound is "drier" and "less sweet" than classical.

In order to play this correctly, greater care has to be taken in the *release action* of the fingers. In this instance the wrist is used to *lift* the hand. This requires intensive thought and listening to duplicate the sound, for instance, that a big band creates.

3) Wrist rotation is often used as a technique to achieve jazz phrasing. The classical player often tries to play jazz arrangements with a fingery technique. This

never works and always sounds incorrect. In jazz, as it is in classical, phrasing is everything. The best way to learn what I am saying is to *listen* to records and copy the phrasing. It is not necessary to know what they are playing, just copy the feel of the music.

4)   The hands (fingers) often do *not* play precisely together. In other words, the style of jazz has a special feel and if you play with the right hand playing precisely with the left hand the music will not "cook", "swing", or have a "groove". I know that many will protest, because through years of classical playing the goal has always been the opposite, but I can assure you that, for instance if the bass player is playing an eighth note walking bass, the piano player will not play precisely with his beats. In fact he will not be playing precisely on the metronomic beat, nor will the drummer. As in tuning a piano with its stretched scale, it is the *precise imperfection* of attacks that gives jazz its special feel.

To practice this, I recommend playing scales and arpeggios just *barely* missing the hands coming down together. Try playing the left hand first, then try playing the right hand first. I know this is painful, but try it. This will be discussed further in the chapter on "Groove Exercises".

5)   Special emphasis on *hand independence* is needed and should be practiced. For instance try just playing a repeated eighth note in the left hand. Then start swinging the right hand in random patterns while trying to keep the left hand playing. After awhile, randomly move the fingers first in the air, then on the piano. Then reverse the hands and play the repeated note in the right hand and wave the left hand in the air.

The rhythmic patterns in the constant hand can be varied. You will probably find that this is harder than you first think and it will take a lot of practice before the hands become free.

There is a center of the brain called the *Corpus Collosum* which organizes the right side and left side activities. In jazz, we often assign different functions to each hand. For instance, the left hand offen functions as "comping" while the right hand solos. If the two hands are in "sync", it severely alters the soloing ideas and the overall "groove". Therefore it is essential that the hands be separate. The masters of this are the drummers since they often have hands and feet totally separate. We have to think as they think.

6) Practice 3 against 2, 2 against 3, 3 against 4 and 4 against 3. This is an extension of the hand independence exercises above. Ideally, when you hear 3 against 2 you hear a *total rhythm*. It is important to perceive the totality, then you will be able to freely improvise within that time frame. Again drummers do this every day and a good idea is to listen to the rhythmic freedom that drummers enjoy.

Many jazz styles, for instance, **Bill Evans**, utilize this 3 against 2 time frame. Drummers who play in this style constantly shift back and forth from three to two. This is similar to the style of **Claude Debussy** where it is important that the music shift effortlessly back and forth between 3 to 2.

There are many ways to practice 3 against 2, but the following is my favorite. Start with the beginning notes of a major scale. Play the triplet in the left hand (or vise versa), which means that you play four notes (the triplet plus one - ie: "C to F"). Play continuously up and down without stopping. Then play the right hand in duple, which means playing three notes (the duplet plus one - ie: "C to E"). When the hands play together, you can say something like, "not diff-icult". Start slowly. If the hands sound mechanical, then try imagining that they are sliding around in butter. Hopefully they will fall into a natural 3 - 2 feel. Then reverse the 3 and 2. Then start randomly reversing back and forth from 3 against 2 to 2 against three. Finally, try improvising using, for instance, an accompaniment pattern in the left hand in three and improvise in the right hand in two. If you can try to freely move back and forth between the two.

The idea is to hear the overall sound that 3 against 2 makes. Once you hear it as a totality, it will be easy to play.

To learn three against four, try the above exercise except saying something like "not ver-y difficult". Three against four is not used as much as three against two, however if you master both, you will find it much easier to play rubato. Also this will help you to achieve certain jazz styles. Once again, listen to drummers!

In general, to develop a good sense of time and rhythm, think like a drummer. Try isolating rhythm from your music. Think only of rhythm by clicking your fingers (always on 2 and 4), beating on your lap or clapping your hands. Take a jazz book, a drummer's manual, or any book which features rhythmic exercises and clap the rhythms. Always play rhythms emotionally, never in a mechanical way. Good rhythm is absolutely essential in jazz.

Finally, It is suggested that you go out and *hear* jazz pianists. Or more correctly, go out and *watch* jazz pianists. Study how they play and how they produce their sound and phrasing. Jazz pianists tend to be more original and different, one from another, than classical pianists because the emphasis on classical is proper technique which leads to a certain amount of conformity.

Many jazz pianists have evolved a technique which works for their style. A classical pianist should be able to study the jazz pianist's style and technique and duplicate it, if he wishes. It is not important that you like the style, it is more important that you study what he does and how he does it.

Technique for Improvisation Review

GENERAL TECHNIQUES FOR IMPROVISATION

1) Have you practiced scales, arpeggios and Hanon using *"Variable Speed"*? **(#1, Page 99)**   Completed: Date_____

2) Have you practiced scales, arpeggios and Hanon using *"Variable Dynamics"*? **(#2, Page 100)**   Completed: Date_____

3) Have you practiced the *"Root, Third, Fifth Arpeggios"*? **(#3, Example 3-1, Pages 100 & 101))**   Completed: Date_____

4) Have you practiced the *"Random Arpeggios"*? **(#4, Page 101)**   Completed: Date_____

5) Have you practiced the *"Random Scales"*? **(#5, Page 102)**   Completed: Date_____

7) Have you practiced the *"Seventh Chord Arpeggios"*? **(#6, Page 103)**   Completed: Date_____

8) Have you worked on and achieved a *beautiful legato*? Is playing with *"weight"* comfortable for you? **(Section 26, Pages 104 - 106)**   Completed: Date_____

9) Did you practice and complete the *"Piano as a Gong"* Exercise? **(Section 27, Page 106)**   Completed: Date_____

10) Did you practice and complete the Rotation Exercise? **(Section 28, Pages 107 & 108)**   Completed: Date_____

11) Have you practiced the *Jazz Technique Exercises*. Are you achieving a proper jazz tone and approach? **(Section 30, Pages 111 - 115)**   Completed: Date_____

12) Have you thought about *"note durations"*?   Completed: Date_____

13) Have you worked on *"Wrist Rotation"*?   Completed: Date_____

14) Have you mastered the special feel which comes from not having the hands come down precisely together. Can you hear it in other jazz pianists?   Completed: Date_____

15) Have you mastered *hand independence*? This may take awhile.   Completed: Date_____

16) Have you mastered the *"three against two"* feel?   Completed: Date_____

17) Make a special effort to *listen to live jazz pianists* to study their technical approach.

Note:

   The purpose of this Chapter is to present ideas, not to lay down rules or "laws". You are encouraged to discover for yourself what makes jazz "tick". This is a music which for generations has been played by "feel". There are many ways that jazz players achieve good feeling.   You are encouraged to enjoy the discovery.

4 Foundations of Jazz Improvisation

The lessons which follow will be much easier and will flow more readily if you have studied and mastered the exercises in the Chapters One and Two. I know that that study in Chapter One, Foundations of Improvisation, was tedious because it dealt primarily with theory, but the study in Chapter Two, Beginning Improvisation, gave you some relief by providing fundamental improvisation exercises. Now that the flow has begun, we are beginning the study of Jazz Improvisation. The transition should be fairly easy *if* you have become comfortable with the beginning chapters. Now the theory becomes more complicated and the style moves into the jazz "dialect" of music language.

Since you are learning jazz improvisation from a book, it is imperative that you *listen* to jazz recordings and hear live jazz performances and then imitate touch, dynamics, phrasing, melody, harmony and rhythm. It is especially important that you write out jazz melodic licks. Then try to play those licks in the same jazz phrasing and feeling as the original. The more that you practice transcription, the better you will become. The idea is not to simply play that one lick exactly as written, but to study the intervals and experiment with it (in all keys) so that you can explore the nature of the language and begin to speak it spontaneously in your soloing.

The purpose of this chapter is, first, to give you a recurring pattern to play so that you can begin to experience motion, rhythm, form and feeling. Once this has established itself into your subconscious, improvising on top of it will be easier. I am saying that it is good to learn to play jazz in stages, learning each stage well. First develop a set of chord changes so that you can play them "in your sleep". It is through the repetition of these chord changes that you will develop the jazz feeling that you need. Then using the correct scale or mode, start making melodies on top of those chord changes. Start by imitating jazz pianists and other instrumentalists. Also try to compose melodies using time honored traditions of melody construction. As said before, pay particular attention to mimicking the touch, phrasing, time and dynamics of good jazz performers. The ability to spontaneously improvise will come from this. You must practice and listen, listen, listen.

31. THE BLUES

We are starting at the source of jazz. The Blues is fun. It is played with simple, honest emotion and should be understood by all jazz players. It is not the purpose of this book to discuss all the blues styles, since the subject has been ably covered in other jazz instruction books. The section of this book entitled *Further Study* will list some jazz instruction books. We are using the blues to help you, the classical player, develop a jazz feel through understanding good time (rhythm), jazz phrasing, developing hand independence, and then to begin to improvise.

The Blues is really two different things, a style and a form. The **Blues Style** is instantly recognizable because it portrays the picture of hard times. It has been portrayed by many vocalists, such as **Billie Holliday, B.B. King, Ray Charles, and Aretha Franklin,** and jazz pianists, trumpet players and guitar players, etc. . When sung, the songs usually tell of troubled relationships and problems. There is a lot of honest feeling in the blues. Often, not always, the blues is played slowly, with sliding notes (blues notes) and short phrases. Blues can also be played in a hard driving upbeat style. Blues is prevalent in styles from dixieland, to swing, to bebop, to today's current rock, fusion, country, and contemporary jazz. There are many many examples of good blues styles on record. It is strongly recommended that you go to a blues club and hear an evening of blues to familiarize yourself with this style of music.

The **Blues Form** relates to a specific set of chord changes over which blues players like to improvise. The patterns are very universal and are known to literally all blues players. The most popular blues form is the *Twelve Bar Blues*. **(See Example 4-1, Page 122)** There are many chord variations on this form and once you have mastered the basic form, it is easy to learn substitute chord progressions.

The Basic 12 Bar Blues Progression should be studied as three groups of four measures. The first group describes the I chord area the next group describes the IV chord area (two measures of IV and two of I) and the final four measures actually describe the V chord, which accomplishes a "turnaround". The turnaround is the ending progression which takes you back to the top (beginning) of the tune. The turnaround will be more fully discussed later in this book.

The purpose of this book is to give you a couple of basic blues progressions so that you can begin to experience the blues form, rhythmic groove and feeling. Also, you can use these blues progressions as a great way to begin right hand soloing. This is just a start. If you want to continue your study of the Blues, there are many variations using chord substitutions. A good list of Blues progressions is found in *Jazz/Rock Voicings for the Contemporary Keyboard Player* by **Dan Hearle**.

EXAMPLE 4-1 BASIC 12 BAR BLUES PROGRESSION

Also the second record, entitled, *Nuthin' But Blues, in A New Approach to Jazz Improvisation for All Instruments* by **Jamey Aebersold** will give you an opportunity to solo with a fine rhythm section. **(See the section on *Further Study*.)**

32. THE BOOGIE WOOGIE BLUES

There are many blues styles which can be performed using this basic progression, but we are going to start with the *Boogie Woogie Blues.* The boogie woogie piano style dates back to the early 1900's, and is distinguished by the left hand *ostinato* or repeated pattern. There are many boogie woogie left hand patterns and in the 1910 - 1930 era, there were many pianists who made their reputation primarily playing the boogie woogie, such as **Gene Ammons, Pine Top Smith and Jelly Roll Morton**. The boogie woogie pattern that I have chosen is simply one of many. If you want to learn more, there are music books which develop this style, but better yet, take them off of records and write them out in your music scrapbook.

I have developed the boogie woogie in the examples in two stages. First, in Step One, we are learning just the open voices **(See Example 4-5, Page 131)**. Learn this, for now in the key of "C". (Of course, you can always learn the examples in all keys.) Then, in Step Two, learn Example 4-6, which is a little more complicated. **(See Example 4-6, Page 132)** The main idea is to learn the *Step Two* pattern until you can literally carry on a conversation while you play it effortlessly.

33. GROOVE TUNES

There are several reasons why I have chosen boogie woogie to begin the jazz improvisation section of this book. This boogie woogie pattern constitutes what I term as a *"Groove Tune"*. A Groove Tune is a tune, or more precisely, a chord progression which is played over and over. Usually the left hand is repeated over and over while the right hand solos. This accomplishes several things. First, it gives you something to play as a *solo* pianist which sounds complete. This is important because many jazz pianists today only play with groups and as a result do not feel comfortable playing solo. I feel that a classical pianist is perhaps most comfortable with solo playing first. It is also important to be a good solo pianist, because then you have a command over all the elements of the music, melody, rhythm and harmony. Then when you add other instruments, they are augmenting your mastery of the parameters of the tune that you are playing.

Secondly, it requires that you, and only you establish the *rhythmic groove*. This "groove" is a term which is usually foreign to the classical player. The term refers to the rhythmic feeling generated by a jazz tune. Remember the phrase, "It don't mean a thing if it ain't got that swing"? This refers to the subliminal message established by the groove. Some jazz players spend more of their energies establishing the groove than others, but all are conscious of it as a major part of the jazz style. Even in a rubato ballad, groove plays an important part of the style.

When you find yourself tapping your foot or snapping your fingers (in jazz, always on 2 and 4, please), you are aware of the groove. A jazz player often tries to make the groove better or deeper as the tune progresses through the choruses. If you play the boogie woogie over and over, eventually you will relax with the pattern until the groove becomes automatic. Then you will notice that your rhythm loosens up as your subconscious takes on more of the duties of controlling the rhythm. At this point you will probably feel the urge to take more liberties with the boogie woogie improvisation. However you must keep the chord pattern consistant.

Listen to players who are considered as good groove players, such as **Oscar Peterson, Monty Alexander and Ahmad Jamal.** Of course, any blues player is considered a groove player. Also listen to big bands, such as **Count Basie.**

So, first play the Stage One boogie woogie example **(See Example 4-5, Page 131)**, and then the Stage Two boogie woogie example **(See Example 4-6, Page 132)** over and over until you can really feel the groove and can completely relax while playing it. Even though the examples are written in 4-4 time, think of them in 12-8 as a rolling three. After awhile, the groove will relax and start to sound like jazz. Listen to the feel that drummers play. **(See Example 4-2)**

EXAMPLE 4-2 TWELVE - EIGHT FEEL OF BOOGIE WOOGIE

Then start adding in *rhythmic chordal patterns* in the right hand and keep the left hand playing the boogie woogie. **(See Examples 4-7 & 4-8, Pages 133 & 134)** Please experiment with *many* different right hand rhythms as you continue your left hand boogie woogie pattern. Listen to blues recordings for ideas. (As said before, you must get your ideas by listening. Blues is often played slowly and is not hard to transcribe and imitate.)

Also inherent in the style are some generalized piano "licks" or sequences usually developed from the *blues scale*. The blues scale is a scale which came quite naturally out of the feelings of the players. In the early days, players did not usually know about scales and simply followed the styles of the day from their ear. Today, we are more prone to study and analyze the styles and thus have developed the term, "blues scale". I mention this because I believe that it is over-stressed and over-used. Today's young rock and jazz players often learn this scale and then let their fingers run wildly up and down the scale without giving much thought to the *melodies* that they are making. The result is a boring, uncontrolled improvisation.

Although, I use the blues scale often, I recommend a slightly different perspective on its use. Instead of thinking of the blues scale as a specific scale, work off of the *mixolydian mode* (which contains the flatted seventh) and liberally add in flatted thirds and flatted fifths. The flat 3, flat 5 and flat 7 can be called "blues notes". The difference is that now you have a better chance to create melodies, much in the same way that the original blues singers and instrumentalists created their blues songs. I also think that this approach should be more appealing to the classical pianist because we are accustomed to making and appreciating good melodies. I suggest listening to blues records and imitating the "licks", trying to maintain the style and inflections. The licks are usually not too difficult to hear and reproduce. Try singing them first, then playing them. Then place them in your improvisation scrapbook. Notice the extensive use of repetitive sequences. **(See Examples 4-8, Page 134)**

Actually, in my personal teaching, I usually do not teach by having the student copy my favorite jazz licks, because this does not encourage the student to improvise on his own. Also, I would rather that the student make a practice of listening to a wide range of blues and jazz musicians of different instruments to develop new discoveries. The student, ultimately, is encouraged to develop his own style based upon a lot of listening and playing. It is important for the student to try to compose tunes and licks and chord progressions etc. Jazz is a music of self discovery. Having said that, I *have* included some blues ideas to help give you are start. Notice that it is popular in the boogie woogie style to alternate in the right hands melody between the thumb and the other fingers. **(See Example 4-9, 135).**

34. BOOGIE WOOGIE EXERCISE

1) Play *Step One Example* until you can play with ease. Notice that we are playing off of the open voicings.

2) Play the *Step Two Example* with the *twelve / eight* feel until you can play totally with ease and you begin to feel the "groove". You do not want a break when you shift from chord to chord. Strive for a good boogie woogie groove. If you play this enough, it will feel like your best friend and your conscious mind will stop control and the subconcious mind will take over. You know that you have established a good groove when, after you have stopped, you can still feel the groove in your body and emotions. Imagine, for fun, that you hear 20,000 people all clapping to your groove (on beats two and four, of course).

3) Next, continue just the left hand as you have been playing in Step Two and start playing *rhythmic chord figures* in the right hand. You can use the examples to get you started, and then add in your own. Again, listen to records for more ideas. It is vitally important that you, as a classical player, start to think rhythmically. Rhythm and rhythmic figures form the foundation of your soloing.

4) Learn the *Blues Scale* and the *Mixolydian*

Mode with the added flat third and fifth. **(See Examples 4-3 & 4-4, Page 131)** Practice playing melodies first without the left hand boogie woogie pattern (to establish phrasing) and then with the left hand. *Put special emphasis on the rhythms that the right hand melodies make.* In other words, listen to, for instance, a big band and clap one of the melodic rhythms. Then go over to the piano and play that one rhythm over and over, making up different melodies from the Mixolydian Mode with the flatted third and fifth. Take special care to *play the phrasing exactly* as the band plays it. You will find that you can create many melodies from that one rhythm. For instance, take one rhythm and play through an entire blues pattern just using that rhythm and altering the melodies.

The importance of these melodic rhythms to the creation of a good sounding jazz solo can not be stressed enough. Even though you can find drum books and other books which deal with these rhythmic licks, it is more important that you find them by listening to records and then adding them to your improvisation scrapbook.

Many classical players have tried and tried to play written jazz solos, only to find that the solos do not sound like the original recordings. I think that the main problems are in the rhythm, touch and phrasing. Often the groove is not correct or is non-existent. For instance, the correct groove in the boogie woogie blues is a 12/8 feel. But that 12/8 is not totally precise and must be learned through listening to blues players. It is a dialect in the language of music.

Also the hands of the classical player are often locked together, right hand and left hand precisely together, which stops the groove and natural feel of the solo. Remember the *hands do not always come down precisely together.* If you listen to a jazz vocalist or instrumental soloist, you will probably not hear them playing in total sync with the rhythm section. There is a sense of rubato to their phrasing.

Also many young jazz students have concentrated on learning jazz scales and modes also without studying melodic rhythms and phrasing only to find that their solos sound like run-on sentences instead of well crafted solos. A solo should have a beginning, a middle and an end. It should "say something". The melodic ideas should follow good melodic principles of tension and release. There should be sequencial and idea development. Also the melodic ideas should always resolve purposefully and cleanly. Then the phrasing will make sense and the ideas will have power.

Listen to the drummers - think like a drummer and you will begin to sound like a jazz player. *Good* drummers have a wonderful sense of rhythmic phrasing. They also think about the groove constantly while they are playing a tune. And, if you are fortunate enough to play with a good drummer, he will feed you many ideas to play. Always try to fit in with his phrasing when you are comping.

Another problem which you will be immediately confronting is *perfecting hand independence.* The left hand pattern must be learned so well that you can literally play any melody in any time frame against it. Of course, the left hand must be establishing the groove and the right hand plays the part of a vocalist or instrumentalist. The soloist (right hand) should be free to *not* have to lay down the groove. He can float over the groove, making melody. This is very difficult to master because the tendency is to play time with the soloing hand. Then, everything locks in and the jazz sounds clunky and un-natural. Listen extensively to great jazz singers like **Sarah Vaughan, Ella Fitzgerald, Nancy Wilson, Mel Torme and Frank Sinatra**, to name just a few. Also, listen to trumpet or sax players to hear how they float over the groove. Mastering this concept and "feel" is essential to developing a good jazz sound.

One way to learn this is to *listen and learn specific licks from a record*, then transfer that to your scrapbook. Now play it on the piano while singing the phrase the way it was originally played or sung. This time do not play the left hand boogie woogie pattern, but rather just play one note in *"stop time"*. Stop time is a term which means that the drummer or the band accents the first beat (or another beat) and the rhythm stops. The soloist solos over this empty space. Then the band punches in on the next first beat, etc. This allows you to hear the basic root tone and to solo with looser phrasing.

Another suggestion is that you try *practicing rubato*, putting all the emphasis on the phrasing of the solo. At this point, do not worry about the groove. Then after you have developed this, add in the left hand boogie woogie pattern, trying to maintain the same phrasing. This is very difficult, but if you persevere, eventually your subconscious will learn this new language. This is a study which you must do for yourself, no amount of written examples will do it for you.

Here are some ideas for soloing. **(See Example 4-10, Page 136)** Choose a rhythmic pattern and play many melodies using it. Change the scales or modes with the chord change, ie. Use C Mixolydian or C Blues with the C7; F Mixolydian or F Blues with the F7, etc. Note: it is also possible to use the C Mixolydian or the C Blues Scale over all the chord changes throughout the blues pattern. Don't forget to add the 12/8 feel throughout. On the same page are several sample endings. **(See Example 4-11, Page 136)** Actually they are variations on a theme. There are many endings which can be used, and as mentioned before, there are many books which deal extensively with these licks.

Have fun, this is just the beginning!

EXAMPLE 4-3   MIXOLYDIAN MODE - WITH ADDED FLAT 3 & 5

Blues Notes

EXAMPLE 4-4 - BLUES SCALE

1   ♭3   4   ♭5   5   ♭7   8 (1)

EXAMPLE 4-5   BOOGIE WOOGIE STAGE ONE

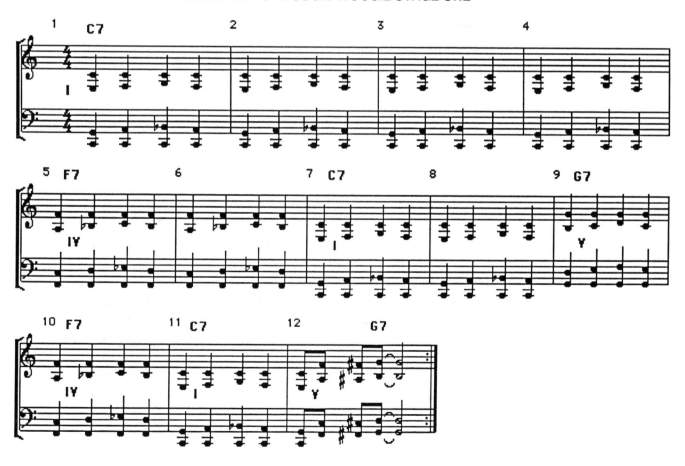

EXAMPLE 4-6   BOOGIE WOOGIE BLUES PART TWO

EXAMPLE 4-7 BOOGIE WOOGIE WITH RHYTHMIC PATTERNS #1

EXAMPLE 4-8 BOOGIE WOOGIE WITH RHYTHMIC PATTERNS #2

EXAMPLE 4-9   BOOGIE WOOGIE BLUES LICK

EXAMPLE 4-10   RHYTHMIC LICK IDEAS

EXAMPLE 4-11   SAMPLE ENDING #1

SAMPLE ENDING #2

SAMPLE ENDING #3

35 TRITONE BLUES

Here is another blues groove tune which features a repeated quarter note figure as the rhythmic ostinato. The figure utilizes the *third and flat seven* of the dominant chord. This interval, a flatted fifth, is also known by the term "tritone". When we delve later into the subject of substitute harmony, you will find many references to this interval. For now we will familiarize ourselves with this interval through playing it in this blues progression.

A brief mention should be made about the use of a common jazz harmonic idea, that of playing a chord 1/2 step above or 1/2 step below as a lead in to a chord. Chromatic chordal movement is very common in jazz. For now, when improvising over the chromatic chords, use the mixolydian mode. Therefore, if the chord is a G7, play a G major scale with a lowered seventh.

It is recommended that you start playing the pattern with the root note played by the left hand and the repeating tritone in the right hand. Play over and over until completely comfortable. Notice that this is a variation from the Boogie Woogie Blues. **(See Example 4-12, Page 139)**

Then play the tritone with the left hand and play rhythmic figures with the right hand, as you did with the boogie woogie. Experiment with different rhythmic patterns. **(See Example 4-13, Page 140)**

Now add in some simple right hand soloing figures while playing the quarter-note tri-tone ostinato in the left hand. **(Example 4-14, Page 141)** For comping practice, try using the right hand rhythmic figures in Example 4-13 in the left hand. Then solo with the right hand. It is difficult to keep the left hand figure going during soloing. It requires excellent hand independence.

This is a good time to mention again the use of "play along" records such as the **Jamey Aebersold Jazz Improvisation Series** of records. The records are very helpful to learn the basics of jazz improvisation; to learn specific styles such as the blues; to learn tunes; and to enjoy the experience of playing along with great players.

The second record of the Series, *Nothing But Blues* is a good method to experience playing blues with a rhythm section. When you listen to the record, especially listen to the pianist's comping. The Tritone Blues will help you as you comp with the left hand. Or you can leave off the left hand and only solo with the right hand.

It is suggested that you choose the slow blues tracks first and learn the progression from the book which accompanies the record. Practice the left hand comping until it is automatic. Start playing some rhythmic figures in the right hand and soloing as described before in the Boogie Woogie Blues section. Work off of rhythmic figures until you are very comfortable with the phrasing. Keep to the Mixolydian and Blues Scale for now. If you have a variable speed tape recorder, try playing the blues in different tempi (and therefore, different keys!).

Incidentally regarding the chords which are not I, IV & V, such as the A7, should be played for now exclusively with the mixolydian mode (flatted seventh). Later, you will use other scales such as the diminished scale over these chords. But, for now you can develop many melodies using the mixolydian mode.

EXAMPLE 4-12 TRITONE BLUES - LEFT HAND BASS, RIGHT HAND OSTINATO TRITONE PATTERN

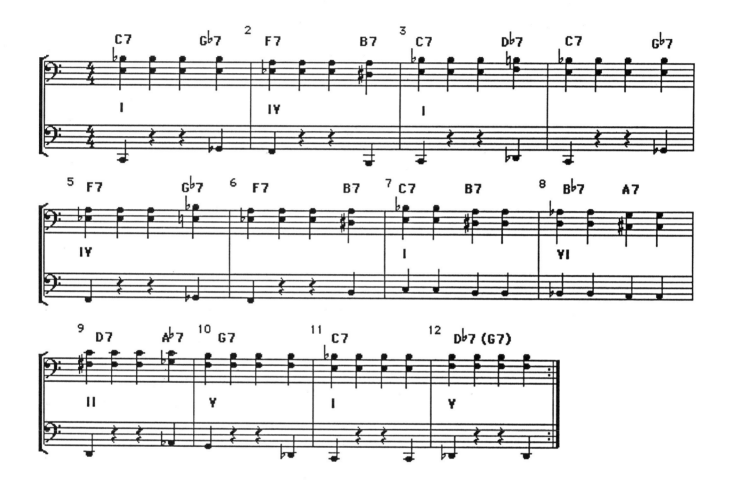

EXAMPLE 4-13 TRITONE BLUES - ACCOMPANIMENT WITH RHYTHMIC FIGURES

EXAMPLE 4-14 TRITONE BLUES - ACCOMPANIMENT IN LEFT HAND

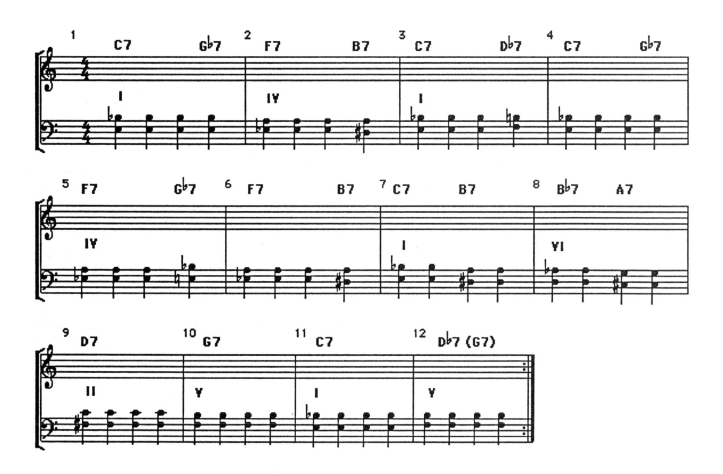

36. CHORD EXTENSIONS

Now we have fully arrived at the area of *Jazz* Theory. If you have ever looked at a jazz fake book, you have noticed chords adorned with extra numbers such as ninths, elevenths and thirteenths. These extensions, counting up from the root, add additional color to the triads and sevenths. Also, in the common practice of leaving out the root when playing extensions, they also add the element of ambiguity which is essential to using jazz substitutions. By and large, it is in the area of extensions that jazz leaves rock and pop. There are some mental tricks, however, that you can learn which will make it easier to master these extensions. The chart below lists the common extensions and their equivalents, one octave lower. **(See Example 4-15)**

EXAMPLE 4-15 - EXTENSION EQUIVALENTS

Extension Equivalents

♭9th·············Minor 2nd

9th············Major 2nd

♯9th·········Minor 3rd

11th·········Perfect Fourth

♯11th·········Tritone (Aug. Fourth)

♭13th·········Flatted Sixth (Aug. Fifth)

13th·········Major Sixth

It is vitally important that you have a facile working relationship with these extensions if you want to play jazz. It will probably take a great deal of perseverence and diligent practice to master the extensions, but it is well worth it.

37. EXTENSION EXERCISE

The best way to learn extensions is to first play and recognize the *third and flat seventh (tritone)*. You must *designate a root tone* in your mind (you do not have to play the root, however). It is relatively easy to spot the third and flat seventh (tritone) in a *dominant style chord*. A dominant style chord is created from the *Mixolydian Mode*, which is a Major Scale with a *flatted seventh*. A commonly played chord using the mixolydian mode is the 9/13 chord. This chord has the 3, flat 7, 9 and 13 (remember, the 9 is one octave up from the 2nd and the 13 is one octave up from the 6th). This chord often plays from V to I. **(See Example 4-16, Page 145)**

For the purpose of this introductory chapter, we are going to use the 9/13 extension which easily applies to the blues which we have been playing. **(See Example 4-16, Page 146)** To ease into the use of extensions, let's start with something that we already know. Take the *Tritone Blues* and *add two additional extension notes* to the tritone. **(See Example 4-17, Page 147)** Note that we are adding a 9th (which is the same as a major second) and a 13th (which is the same as a 6th). Now explore the blues, this time using the chord extensions in the left hand. This should sound good with the *Aebersold Record Number 2, Blues Record*. Use the Mixolydian Mode and blues scales to improvise over these chords. This is a good opportunity to start to play in other keys, eventually *all keys*.

In the future when you play the third and flat seventh, practice *adding in two other extensions* to the chord. As in other exercises in this book, you should *invent* many many chords on your own. To give you some other examples, I have included some other commonly used extensions. **(See Example 4-16, Page 145)** Also, for a more complete look at extensions, turn to **Chapter 6, Section 59, Chord Alterations, Extensions and Tonalities, Page 209.** Make sure that you label each chord with the extensions that you are using. When labeling extensions, remember you usually do not have to list the seventh or the third. It is convenient to include these extensions as part of the II,V,I Progression **(See Section 38, Pages 148 - 153.)**

EXAMPLE 4-16   COMMONLY PLAYED DOMNANT EXTENSIONS

First recognize the tri-tone

EXAMPLE 4-17 TRITONE BLUES USING EXTENSIONS/QUARTER NOTE OSTINATO

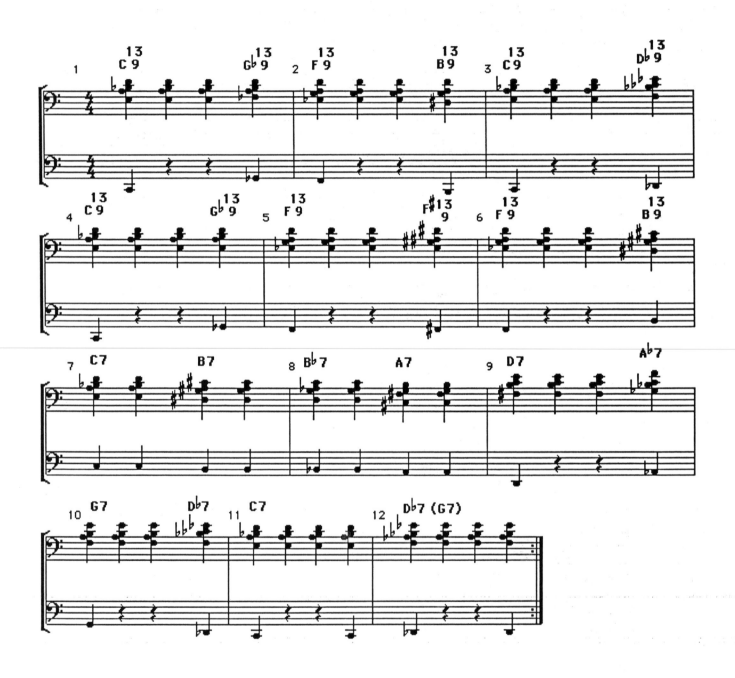

EXAMPLE 4-18 TRITONE BLUES WITH EXTENSIONS - COMPING LEFT HAND

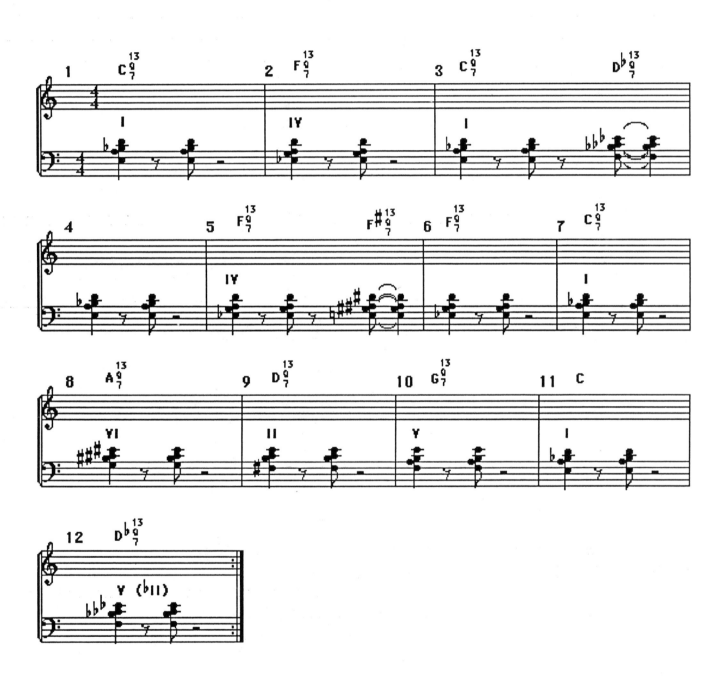

38. II V I PROGRESSION

This progression is perhaps the very foundation of jazz. It is impossible to overrate its importance. Perhaps you have already noticed the irresistible power of the V - I progression. This has a great deal to do with the resolution of the 3 and the 7. The 3 of the G7 wants to resolve to the 1 of the I chord, C. And the Flat 7 of the G7 chord wants to resolve to the 3 of the I chord. As we travel around the Cycle of Fourths (Flats), we are constantly moving from V to I (ie. G to C). Also, if we travel from D to G to C, as we would around the Cycle of Fourths, we are continuing this V to I twice. This is the II, V, I Progression and it forms the basis of most jazz tunes. Along with completely knowing the Cycle of Keys itself, the II, V, I probably represents the single most important basic knowledge in the study of jazz. **(See Example 4-19, Page 150)**

This II,V,I exercise can be practiced in many different ways. The progression should be played around the Cycle of fourths and fifths (Flats and Sharps) **(See Examples 4-19 & 4-20, Pages 150 & 151)** and also up and down chromatically. It should also be practiced using a II, V, I in minor. **(See Example 4-21, Page 152).**

1.) Start with the examples as shown with the left hand playing the roots and the right hand playing the chord.

2) Then play with the left hand playing the chord and sing the roots.

Now, the real secret to learning progressions is to learn them in *all* inversions and also in *open voicings*. **(See Example 4-22, Page 153)** Some jazz instruction books suggest that you learn the first and third positions only, but I feel that since each position or inversion contains different melody notes on top, *you should learn all of the positions.* I realize that it is very time consuming to learn this progression in all ways, but since the accompanying left hand must be playing almost automatically, you must have it totally commited within your subconscious. The best advice is to start your study of progressions early in your study and stick with it until you are an expert!

EXAMPLE 4-19   BASIC II V I PROGRESSION IN MAJOR

EXAMPLE 4-20 BASIC II V I PROGRESSION IN MAJOR

Sharp Direction

EXAMPLE 4-21   BASIC II V I PROGRESSION IN MINOR

EXAMPLE 4-22   BASIC II V I OPEN VOICINGS PROGRESSION IN MAJOR

Flat Direction

39. MODAL SOLOING

In the chapter on Foundation of Improvisation, we discussed the modes and you were given some beginning exercises in Modal Improvisation. The modes can also be used to learn to solo over the II, V, I Progression. The three modes that you will use in the Major II, V, I, will be the *Dorian Mode (Flat 3 and 7)*, over the II chord, the *Mixolydian Mode (Flat 7)* over the V chord; and the *Ionian Mode (Major Scale)* over the I chord. Practice playing each of these modes separately, until you know them very well. Then apply them to the II, V, I progression. **(See Examples 4-23 & 4-24, Page 155)**

40. EXERCISE - II, V, I SOLOING WITH RIGHT HAND

1) Put on a metronome or a drum machine at a comfortable (preferably, slow) tempo. Start playing the left hand comping using the II, V, I.

2) Then start soloing with the right hand. Try to *think of the modes* as you shift between the Dorian, Mixolydian and Ionian. If you can not improvise "on the fly", try *composing* simple melodies at first. Don't forget to use melodic rhythmics as you solo. The *Jamey Aebersold Records, Record #3 on the II, V, I* will be very helpful at this point. Play around the cycle, both ways.

3) Reverse the hands and play the II, V, I in the right hand and solo in the left hand. Leave off the II, V, I and exchange solos between the hands - four bars to each hand. Note: *Do not neglect the left hand!*

4) Try soloing *without* an accompaning hand. Then trade solos, first with right hand, then with the left. This is a difficult exercise.

EXAMPLE 4-23 II, V, I SHOWING PATTERN FOR MODAL SOLOING

EXAMPLE 4-24 SHOWS MODES USED FOR MODAL SOLOING ON II, V, I

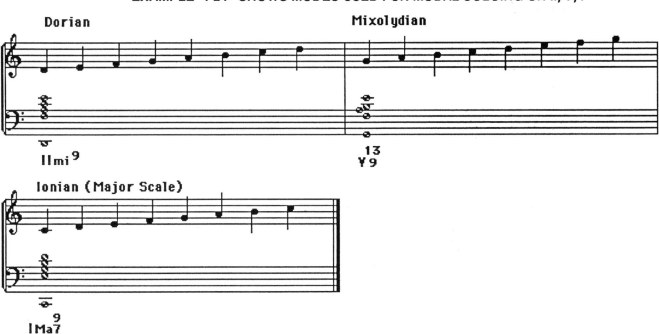

Foundations of Jazz Improvisation Review

THE BLUES

1)   Do you have an understanding of the *Blues Style*? **(Page 119)**

Completed: Date_____

2)   Do you know the *12 Bar Blues* as given in **Example 4-1, Page 122?**

Completed: Date_____

3)   Do you have an understanding of the concept of *"Groove Tunes"* and the overall concept of the groove? **(Page 123)**

Completed: Date_____

4)   Can you easily play the *Stage One Example of the Boogie Woogie Blues*? **(Example 4-5, Page 131)**

Completed: Date_____

5)   Can you easily play the *Stage Two Example of the Boogie Woogie Blues*? **(Example 4-6, Page 132)**

Completed: Date_____

6)   Do you know the *Blues Scale* in "C"? Do you know the Blues Scale in all keys? Do you understand the concept of the *Mixolydian Mode with added flat 3, & 5*? **(Example 4-3, Page 131)**

Completed: Date_____

7)   Can you play the *Boogie Woogie with rhythmic patterns #1*. **(See Example 4-7, Page 133)**

Completed: Date_____

8)   Can you play the *Boogie Woogie with rhythmic patterns #2*. **(See Example 4-8, Page 134)** Have you experimented with your own rhythmic patterns?

Completed: Date_____

9)   Can you play the *Boogie Woogie Blues Lick* ? **(Example 4-9, Page 135)**

Completed: Date_____

10) Can you play the *Boogie Woogie Blues with different rhythms*? **(Example 4-10, Page 136)**

Completed: Date_____

11) Can you play the *Sample Endings* ? Have you tried to create your own Blues endings? **(Example 4-11, Page 136)**

Completed: Date_____

12) Have you mastered the *Tritone Blues* with the left hand bass, right hand ostinato? **(Example 4-12, Page 139)**

Completed: Date_____

13) Have you mastered the *Tritone Blues with Rhythmic Figures* in the right hand? **(Example 4-13, Page 140)**

Completed: Date_____

14) Have you mastered the *Tritone Blues with the left hand tritone*? Practice the Continuous Eighth Note Exercise using the Blues Scales and the Mixolydian Scale? Then start soloing using Blues Phrases. **(Example 4-14, Page 141)** This will take some time. Please read the section on Blues carefully.

Completed: Date_____

CHORD EXTENSIONS

15) Have you memorized the *Extension Equivalents* in **(Example 4-15, Page 142)?**

Completed: Date_____

16) Have you thoroughly practiced the *Extension Exercise* ? This exercise will take a long time to master. **(Example 4-16, Pages 143 -145)**

Completed: Date_____

17) Did you practice the *Tritone Blues using Extensions?* **(Example 4-17, Page 146)**

Completed: Date_____

18) Did you practice the *Tritone Blues using Extensions in the comping left hand*? **(Example 4-18, Page 147)**

Completed: Date_____

II, V, I PROGRESSION

19)   Did you master the *II, V, I progression around the flat direction* of the Cycle of Keys? This will take a long time, but is essential to your study. **(Example 4-19, Page 150)**

Completed: Date_____

20)   Did you master the *II, V, I progression around the sharp direction* of the Cycle of Keys? This will also take a long time. **(Example 4-20, Page 151)**

Completed: Date_____

21)   Did you master the *Minor II, V, I progression around the flat direction* of the Cycle of Keys? This will also take a long time. **(Example 4-21, Page 152)**

Completed: Date_____

22)   Did you master the *II, V, I progression around the flat direction* of the Cycle of Keys in *open voicings*? This will take a long time. **(Example 4-22, Page 153)**

Completed: Date_____

23)   Did you practice *Modal Soloing over the II, V, I*? **(Examples 4-23 & 4-24, Page 155)**

Completed: Date_____

Note: Hang in there! This chapter represents a start. However the "start" will demand practice and listening. Try to find other musicians to "jam" with. Trade "licks" with another musician. Accompany vocalists and instrumentalists. Good Luck!

5 Foundations of a Tune

Finally, we are at a point where we can actually learn to improvise and create our *own arrangement* on a *tune*, a song, a piece of music. We want to be able to improvise a jazz solo. We want to be able to spontaneously accompany a singer or instrumentalist. Most importantly we want to be able to sit down and create a beautiful solo arrangement in our *own style*. Please remember, that the preparatory work you have been doing up until this time, will now come to fruition. It is important to have a good approach to learning a tune. This trains your mind to think in certain ways. If you do this haphazardly, the results lead to sloppy improvisation. Also, all good musicians have a way that they think about a tune. This is part of the language of music. As with the other chapters, it is important that you *practice each step until the step is automatic.* Also it will be helpful if you will include all of your learned tunes in your notebook. As you learn new harmonic, melodic or rhythmic ideas, you can add them to your tune.

41. LEARNING A TUNE

There are many sources from which to learn a tune. Of course, the most obvious choice is to go to the original music, usually in sheet music form. Even though this is the most basic source, it might not be the preferred place to go. Certainly it is important to see a tune written as it is originally intended, but since jazz tunes are seldom played in their original style, with the original chords, etc., you must look to other sources. Most importantly, you should listen to recorded and live versions of the tune. If it is a jazz tune, or a tune which is often played by jazz players, you can often find it in a Fake Book. A Fake Book is a compilation of tunes with the melody and chords written. Often, more information is also given, such as countermelodies, special riffs (jazz melodic ideas), alternate chord changes, special bass lines and lyrics.

Perhaps, the best method of learning a tune is to use a combination of all sources. However, of the various ways to learn a tune, I personally like listening to recorded versions by pianists whom I like. After writing the tune down, then I like to create my own arrangement. I often change the chords, rhythms and melody to come up with a personalized arrangement. It is particularly fun to hear a tune which has been played many ways by different musicians.

Write your tune out so that the *bass line* and *melody* are clear. Actually a distinction should be made between *chord structure* and *bass line*. The chord structures are the harmonic changes and the chord types which flow through the tune. The bass line is the actual line that the bass player plays. Sometimes the bass line is not the root, as in a "G/B" which indicates that you have a "G chord" with a "B" in the bass.

In your first version of writing out the tune, especially if you are listening to a recorded version, it is recommended that you first listen to the *bass line*. It is easier to hear and then you have the foundation notes of the tune (however, not necessarily the root of the chord). Then, write the melody, which is also easy to hear.

Then, write the chord changes in the key that you are writing the song. Include the chord type, such as major seventh, minor seventh, etc. This is much more difficult to hear. I recommend that you listen first for the type of triad. See if you can hear major, minor, augmented or diminished. If not, listen for the root of the chord and try to hear the third and/or flat seventh. From there, listen for extensions such as the flat ninth, sharp eleventh etc. Finally, listen for the type of scale which fits that chord. For instance listen for the flatted seventh and the mixolydian mode, or the minor third and flat seventh to hear the dorian mode.

Finally, list the *numbers* of the chord changes, such as I, IV, V, etc. To do this you first write down the bass line. Then list the chord. Finally try to determine the *root*. Once you have decided on the root, you can set up the chord changes, written in roman numerals, ie: I, IV, V, etc. This will enable you to play and hear the tune in any key. Notice that the chord changes have been clustered around II,V,I. In jazz we often think of tunes in series of II, V's and, in our mind, we are experiencing mini key changes. If we then can remember the interval relationship between the mini key changes, we can then easily play the song in any transposition. **(See Example 5-1, Page 168)**

42. EXERCISE IN LEARNING A TUNE

1) Notice the *form* of the tune. When you write out the tune, try to block out the sections so that they are clear. For instance, make sure that the Bridge is clearly defined and that first and second endings are delineated. **(See Example 5-1, Page 168)**

2) Learn and write the *melody*. One way to really get to know a melody is to play the melody in all keys. You have to use a combination of knowing the intervals and using your ears. If you can, play just the melody of *Eliza* or a tune of your choice in all keys, you will really start to know the tune. Try to think of the intervals of the melody, especially the interval of the starting note. It is a good exercise to play lots of melodies from memory and then play them in all keys. **(See Example 5-1, Page 168)**

3) Explore different ways to "swing" the melody. Jazz players take great liberties with the notes and the rhythm of the melody. Even though it is written "straight" as in Example 5-1, a jazz player will automatically create a jazz feeling by altering the melody. Example 5-2 gives one example of this. Notice how many different ways the melody can be syncopated. **(See Example 5-2, Page 170)**

4) Learn and write the *bass line.* Write and play it in whole and half notes. Remember, that sometimes the bass note will not be the root note, but an alternative which gives a better voicing of the chord or better voice leading for the bassist.

5) Play the melody along with the bass line playing in half and whole notes. This allows you to hear the harmonic structure from the top and bottom of your arrangement. For the purposes of jazz improv, it is very important that you hear the tune from the perspective of the bass player. **(See Examples 5-1 & 5-2, Pages 168 - 171)**

6) While still playing the basic melody in the right hand, start playing *"lead-in" notes* in the bass line. The lead-in notes can be a whole or half step above or below the note you are heading toward. Sometimes they can be chord tones. Experiment with different lead-ins. **(See Example 5-3, Page 172)**

7) After you are proficient in playing the lead-in notes in the bass, add in more lead-in notes until you can play *continuously in quarter notes.* Now you have a *Walking Bass Line.* The concept of lead-in notes is important since, in improvisation, you always want to know *where you are going with your musical ideas.* For instance, it is crucial that you not embark on a musical idea without knowing where that idea will land. Many players do not have this kind of control in improvisation.

This often results in faulty phrasing because the player does not know where the phrase will end. Overall, this usually means that the ideas will lack conviction and power.

If the bass line is correctly organized, this sets up the right hand improv. You can hear the bass line as a roadway which connects the chords. In other words, instead of the chords being static entities, you perceive a connection as you leave one chord and move into another. This makes the entire right hand solo more understandable. Incidentally, it should be mentioned that later on, when you play your finished improvisation, you possibly or even probably will not actually play the bass line on the piano, however, you will hear it in your head, or possibly have a bass player to play the lines. **(See Example 5-4, Page 174)**

This stage is very difficult since the bass line should not be the same each time. In other words, practice it with left hand alone so that you can lead into the chords in different ways. For instance, sometimes, come in diatonically or chromatically from above and sometimes from below. Try different ways to melodically move from one chord to another.

The bass line, however, should not be played in a melodic manner. Instead, it should take on the *function of the bass player* in a rhythm section. It is advised that you start *listening* to records and live jazz bands to hear the concept of the bassist. His function is largely rhythmic and the bass lines are not to be construed in a melodic way but as a tension moving to a resolution (the next chord.).

Also, it is absolutely necessary that when playing with a walking bass line the right hand and left hand *not play precisely together.* They must play just slightly off, either before or after. I know this is a difficult concept for a classical player to swallow. You have to listen very carefully to a jazz trio, piano, bass and drums to hear what I mean. If the hands always play together, the piece will sound like a Bach piece, instead of a jazz tune. In order to get a "feel" into your music, the hands should play slightly, not noticeably, off. After a great deal of listening and playing, you will develop this feel.

Also, the notes are *not* played precisely on the beat. Both the bass line and the melody are slightly off. Again, you will have to study this for yourself to develop the right "feel".

8) After the walking bass line is mastered, start *comping* in the right hand while *"walking"* in the left hand. You can use the voicings of II, V, I that you learned in the last chapter. In this tune, you have both II, V, I in major and in minor. **(See Example 5-5, Page 176)** Experiment with different *inversions* of the extension voicings in the right hand. This step also should take time to master. Try different ways to play the progressions. Then try playing the comping chords only in the left hand (without playing the right hand at all). This is the normal function of the left hand when the pianist plays with a bass player. It takes a great deal of experience to comp with the left hand so that it is totally independent from the right hand soloing.

9) To start to improvise off of the melody, it is advised that you again simplify the left hand to half and whole notes so that your full attention can go to the soloing hand. Next, in the melody, we should pick certain melodic notes which we will call *"destination notes"*. In the case of *Eliza,* to start we will arbitrarily choose the first note of each measure. Now similarly to the walking bass line, *we will head for these destination notes*. In the following example several ideas will be given to arrive at the "G". **(See Examples 5-6 & 5-7, Pages 178 & 179)**

The *destination notes* are your choice. However it is important that you always have these points of resolution. If you don't, your improv will sound aimless and will not have proper phrasing. *It is most important that you be aware of the rhythm leading up to the Destination Note.* For instance, in the Example 5-6, there is a half note and two quarter notes leading to the Destination Notes. It is a wonderful exercise to *change those rhythms*, then play the same rhythm to each of the Destination Notes. In this way you have to build your melodic notes *around the rhythm*. You hear the rhythm first, then attach a melodic idea to it. Practice beating a rhythmic fragment, then playing it through the tune, over and over, using different melodies ending on the Destination Notes. **(See Example 5-7, Page 178)**

Speaking of phrasing, you should practice your melodic routes with different phrasing and timing. In jazz, as in classical, *we phrase everything.* However in jazz, we often experiment with *different timing in phrases*. The only way to understand what I am saying is to listen to lots and lots of players. Carefully analyze their phrasing and try to perform exactly as they do. Especially listen to vocalists, since they are the masters of phrasing. Many pianists actually think of the lyrics of a song to try to find the "right" phrasing. Also, it is strongly advised that you sing along with your soloing.

Make an exercise out of *arriving at the destination notes*, and trying many ways of phrasing to arrive at those notes. Work on one destination note at a time. This will take some time. Keep at it until you can do it spontaneously.

As another exercise try playing straight through the tune, spontaneously improvising using a *continuous eighth note solo.* Next try continuous eighth note triplets, and finally continuous sixteenth notes. When you are really competent at playing all time values, then start mixing them up. Finally add in *space*. I often practice by playing continuous soloing just to get my subconscious "rolling". Also I want to establish the "hook-up" between my brain and my hands. Sometimes the flow is there, sometimes not. Of course, after awhile, I start adding space and phrasing into the soloing.

43. BALLAD STYLE

9) To develop a *ballad style* of playing, where the piano is played in a fuller style, try practicing *"Stop on the the Chord"*. "Stop on the Chord" is an extension of the Modal Exercise given in the chapter on Beginning Improvisation **(See Pages 82-85)**. For instance, play *Eliza* and stop at the first "D Minor" chord. Now pretend that time has stopped for an instant and freely improvise on "D Dorian". Just play on and on, with no particular relation to *Eliza.*

Then move on to the "G7 chord" and play on the G Mixolydian Mode for awhile. The more you practice this exercise, you will begin to find different avenues to play through the modes of *Eliza.* Try not to play cliche accompaniments and stay away from standard chords, such as triads. To do this play more *major seconds and perfect fourths*. When you improvise, always establish some rhythm. Try different combinations of notes together. In other words, *make up your own chords.*

This is a very valuable exercise and should be practiced eventually *in all keys.* In fact, it is highly recommended that you start playing *Eliza* in all keys. Remember that the tune is primarilly made up of II, V, I. Practice all the steps as given in this exercise.

Remember, you can use the *Dorian Mode* (flat 3 and 7) over the II minor chord; the *Mixolydian Mode* (flat 7) over the V7 chord; and the *Ionian Mode* (Major Scale) over the I major. In the II, V, I in the minor, use the *Locrian Mode* (Flat 2, 3, 5, 6, 7) over the II minor 7 flat 5; the *diminished scale* (hasn't been presented yet) over the V7 flat 9; and the *Dorian, Phrygian, Aeolian Modes or Melodic Minor Scale* over the I minor.

As suggested before, it is important to always choose a *melodic rhythm* to solo with. Think of the melodic rhythm, then apply the appropriate mode or scale to the rhythm. Work on phrasing, getting the jazz feel, good melodic construction and, in general, getting a good jazz sound on the piano. Try not to ramble on and on. **(See Example 5-7, Page 178)**

"Stop on the Chord" is a principle method of developing a ballad style. The more you practice this exercise you will discover many ways to play a tune, texturally, rhythmically and melodically. Listen to good jazz ballad pianists such as **Bill Evans, Denny Zeitlin, Chick Corea, George Shearing, Oscar Peterson and Monty Alexander** to discover the many approaches to playing a ballad. This is where the solo pianist and also the classical pianist can fully exhibit his skills. This is where classical skills such as tone, phrasing, dynamics, line, balance and all manner of interpretation can come fully into play.

Do not assign your hands to specific roles such as left hand, accompaniment and right hand solo. Do not fall into playing accompaniment patterns over and over. Also do not always play chords in their root positions. Explore seconds and fourths and chord fragments. The chapter on Advanced Theory will further explore this area.

One problem that classical players have when playing a ballad is to not think in terms of a rhythmic groove. Even though the style is mellow and quiet, the rhythmic intensity should still be there. Don't let it sag in the middle and become soapy. Again, the best way to describe a good ballad is to suggest that you listen to good players.

EXAMPLE 5-1   ELIZA - MELODY AND SIMPLE BASS LINE

Eliza

Martan Mann
May 31, 1988

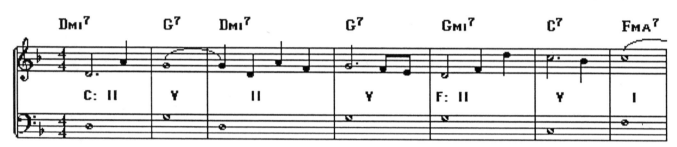

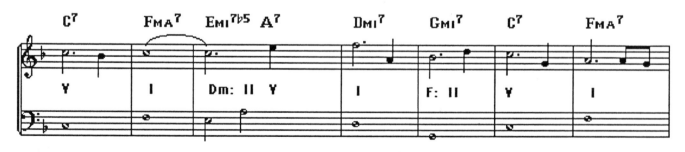

EXAMPLE 5-2 ELIZA - SYNCOPATED MELODY AND SIMPLE BASS LINE

Eliza

Martan Mann
May 31, 1988

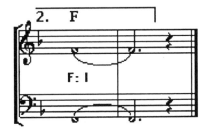

EXAMPLE 5-3 ELIZA - BASS LINES WITH LEAD-INS

Eliza

Martan Mann
May 31, 1988

EXAMPLE 5-4 ELIZA WITH WALKING BASS LINE

Eliza

Martan Mann
May 31, 1988

EXAMPLE 5-5 ELIZA - RH COMPING, LH WALKING BASS

EXAMPLE 5-6 ELIZA - MELODIC IMPROV TO FIRST DESTINATION NOTE

EXAMPLE 5-7 ELIZA - DIFFERENT MELODIC RHYTHMS FOR SOLOING

1.

2.

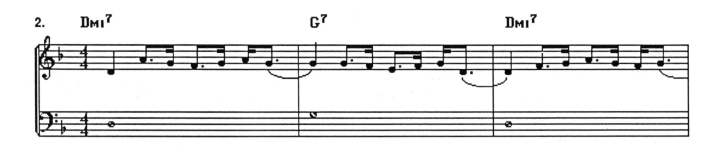

3.

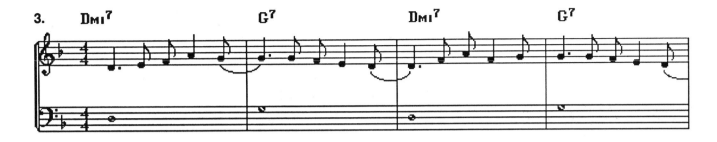

4.

5.

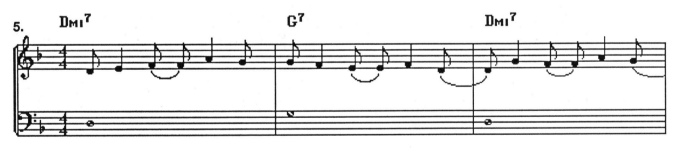

Foundations of a Tune - Review

WRITING OUT A TUNE

1) Did you *write out the Melody*? Have you studied the intervals so that you can play the melody in all keys? **(Section 41, Pages 159 - 160 & Example 5-1, Page 168)**

Completed: Date_____

2) Did you *write out and play the Bass Line* in half and whole notes? **(Section 41, Pages 159 - 160 & Examples 5-1 & 5-2, Pages 168 - 171)**

Completed: Date_____

3) Did you *write out the Chords*? Have you listened for the type of triad? the type of seventh? type of extension? **(Section 41, Pages 159 - 160 & Example 5-1, Page 168)**

Completed: Date_____

4) Did you *write out the Chord Progression* (Roman Numerals)? **(Section 41, Pages 159 - 160 & Example 5-1, Page 168)**

Completed: Date_____

Of course, you can write out *many* tunes of your choice in this way.

LEARNING A TUNE

6) Did you *play the Melody*? Did you learn it by intervals so that you can play it in all keys? **Example 5-1, Pages 168 & 169)**

Completed: Date_____

6)   Did you practice "swinging" the melody? Try different syncopations. **(Example 5-2, Pages 170 & 171)**

Completed: Date_____

7)   Did you *play* the Melody along with the Bass Line (Bass Line playing in half and whole notes)? **(Examples 5-1 & 5-2, Pages 168 - 171)**

Completed: Date_____

8)   Did you practice playing "lead-ins" into the Bass Lines? Can you do this while playing the basic melody? Also, can you spontaneously find different lead-ins? **(Example 5-3, Pages 168 & 169)**

Completed: Date_____

9)   Did you learn and perfect playing *Walking Bass Lines*? (This will take a long time.) Don't forget to make the Bass Line sound like it was played by a Bass Player. Can you play these Walking Bass Lines while playing a *simple* Melody? Are your hands *not* together? **(Example 5-4, Pages 174 & 175)**

Completed: Date_____

10)   Next practice *comping with the right hand while doing a Walking Bass Line with the left hand.* Use different inversions in the right hand extensions. Try the examples using different rhythmic patterns. **(Example 5-5, Pages 176 & 177)**

Completed: Date_____

11)   Now *improvise with the right hand* while playing half and whole notes in the bass. Practice arriving at "Destination Notes" using the Examples 5-6 & 5-7. Make up your own rhythmic patterns to play. This exercise will and should take some time. **(Examples 5-6 & 5-7, Pages178 & 179)**

Completed: Date_____

12)   Play the *Continuous Eighth Note Exercise* until you can play with complete control. Also play Continuous Eighth Note Triplets and Continuous Sixteenth Notes. Now mix them. Now insert space and phrasing. This exercise should take some time.

Completed: Date_____

13)   Practice *"Stop on the Chord"* until you know the modes very well. Practice developing a Ballad Style.   Completed: Date_____

Note:

This Chapter has far-reaching importance. Although I have presented just "Eliza" for your study, you can apply these principles to any tune. Seek out tunes which you would like to learn, write them and learn them. Constantly expand your repertoire. The next chapter will give you more advanced ideas for your arrangements. Good luck.

6 Advanced Theory

In the prior chapter, Foundations of a Tune, you learned the basics of how to put together an improvisation or a basic arrangement of a Tune. In this chapter, we will go much further in exploring possibilities of dressing up *Eliza* or any other tune that you wish to explore. As said many times in this book, this chapter will be much easier if you have diligently practiced the ideas presented in earlier chapters.

44. CHORD SUBSTITUTIONS AND ALTERATIONS

A tune can sound reasonably well with the standard changes, but in jazz, it is universally accepted that you have license to substitute and alter the chords. The alteration of chords relates to the *changing of the chord type*, for instance from major to minor, or from a major seventh to a dominate seventh. In doing so, we are also *altering the scale* that we are using for soloing. Chord alterations and different scales will be discussed shortly, but for now we will discuss *chord substitutions, which means to substitute one chord for the original.*

45. TRITONE SUBSTITUTION

By far the most often used chord substitution in jazz is the *Tritone Substitution*. Once you begin to master this substitution, you will start to understand much of what you hear in jazz. This tritone substitution is used over and over. It is the foundation of most intros, turnarounds, and many endings of songs. It is a convenient way to modulate to a new key. And, it is a primary method of jazz soloing and comping. Bass players freely utilize this substitution.

To start, let's return to the Blues and the tritone accompaniment. Remember, we played the third and the flat seventh (tritone) as the primary intervals in the dominant seventh chord. It is interesting that if you play a third and seventh, let's say "B" and "F", the root is "G". Now if we exchange the root for a "D Flat", which is a tritone away from "G", now the "B" and "F" are reversed. The "B" is the seventh and the "F" is the third. This is another way of pointing out that both "G" and "D Flat" share two of the same notes (in reverse). **(See Example 6-1)**

EXAMPLE 6-1   TRITONE SUBSTITUTION

This means that in many cases, not all, if you see a "G7" on the chart, you can substitute a "D Flat7" for it. Keep in mind that this works for some styles of jazz. It definitely does not work in other styles such as Country Western, pop and rock. Also, a major determining factor of whether or not the tritone substitution will work, is the melody of the tune. Sometimes you have to change the melody to make it work, or simply not use that kind of substitution.

46. THE TURNAROUND

The best way to practice the tritone substitution is within the structure of the *turnaround.*. If you will remember, the final four bars of the blues was referred to as the "turnaround". The turnaround, as its name implies is the area of the tune which returns the tune back to the beginning of a section, or carries it on to the next section, such as in the case of the "Bridge". Very often, the intro can also be a turnaround and sometimes, the ending is a turnaround. If the turnaround repeats over and over, without a set place to stop, this is known as a "vamp".

A very common turn around is the "Heart and Soul" or "We want Cantor" vamp of I, VI, II, V. In its most natural form, within the key, it is written as I major, VI minor, II minor, and V7 dominant. **(See Example 6-2)**

EXAMPLE 6-2   I, VI, II, V7 TURNAROUND

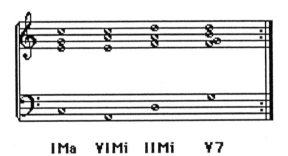

IMa   VIMi   IIMi   V7

To more clearly understand and hear the tritone substitution, we will only use the dominant form and only use the 3 and Flat 7. **(See Example 6-3)**

EXAMPLE 6-3- I, VI, II, V USING DOMINANT CHORDS

The examples which follow will give some variations which you will find as you use the tritone substitutions. For instance, if the second chord is an "A", which is the sixth, it can be substituted by an "E Flat", which is a tritone away. By doing this, you can have many combinations. Note the relationship of fourths and also chromatic half steps. The I chord has been substituted by the III and it's tritone sub, the Flat VII. The III is the next chord around the Cycle of Keys. Therefore it is natural to use E, A, D, G, to C. (or III, VI, II, V, I).

Practice these substitutions extensively, in all keys, until you can play and hear them automatically. Then, start inserting them into the Blues and other tunes that you are learning. Incidentally many jazz tunes use this turnaround-tri-tone substitution combination and call the pattern "Rhythm Changes". The term, "Rhythm Changes" comes from the tune, "I've Got Rhythm". You can practice a walking bass line and improvise in the right hand using different combinations of rhythm changes. Also try making up different intros and endings using these changes. **(See Example 6-4)**

EXAMPLE 6-4   VARIATIONS OF THE TRITONE SUBSTITUTION

1.

2.

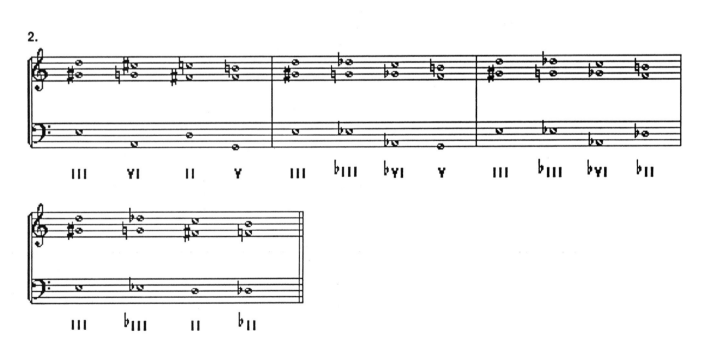

3.

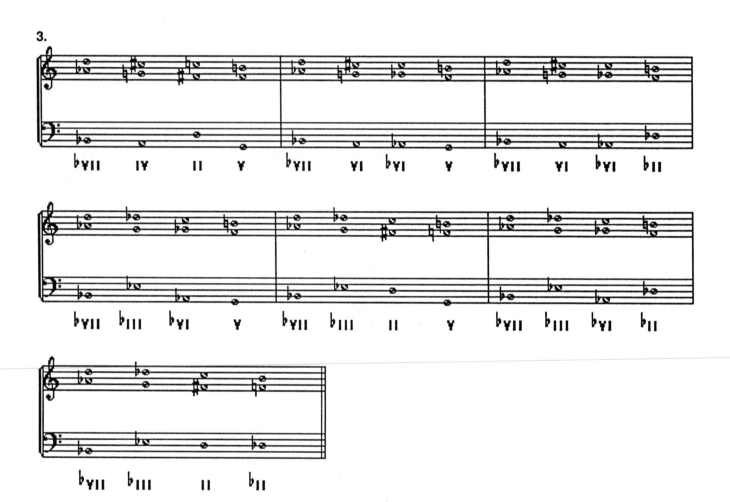

$\flat$VII IV II V $\flat$VII VI $\flat$VI V $\flat$VII VI $\flat$VI $\flat$II

$\flat$VII $\flat$III $\flat$VI V $\flat$VII $\flat$III II V $\flat$VII $\flat$III $\flat$VI $\flat$II

$\flat$VII $\flat$III II $\flat$II

47. DIMINISHED SCALE AND COLOR CHORDS

The *Diminished Scale* and *"Color Chords"* will instantly dress up your chords and melodic soloing. Also, given the nature of the diminished scale as an "equal distant scale", it is very easy to learn and hear. The diminished scale is built around the minor third intervals which make up the diminished seventh chord. These minor third intervals are equally proportioned from octave to octave. The scale can be constructed as a *half-whole or a whole half diminished.* **(See Example 6-6)**

The Diminished Scale, because of the equal distance, only has three different keys. If you play the "C Diminished", "C Sharp or D Flat Diminished", and "D Diminished", you have learned *all* the scales because "E Flat Diminished" is the same scale as "C Diminished". Learn to play the diminished scales in all keys. Also, the "Whole Half and Half Whole Diminished are, in reality the same scale because if, for example, you start a "Half/Whole C Diminished Scale" on the *second degree* of that scale, you will be playing a "D Whole/Half Diminished Scale". So actually, you only have three different scales to learn, "C", "C Sharp or D Flat", and "D".

The scales should be played with two hands until thoroughly known. The Diminished Scale is primarily used while playing either a dominant or diminished chord. In this case, the player thinks of a Whole/Half Diminished Scale off of the Flatted Ninth of the dominant chord. Notice the extensions which fall into this scale and which extensions that do not. For instance, you can play the Flat 9, and Sharp 9, but not the Major 9th. The Sharp 11 and 13th works but the flat 13 does not. The scale works very well with the diminished seventh chord. To be completely safe, you can just play the tritone 3 and flat 7 chord in the left hand. The Sharp 11, Flat 9 chord works well and also happens to be the tritone substitution dominant chord. If you are playing *Eliza,* the diminished works very well with the E7 Flat 9 in Measure 16, since it moves to a minor chord. **(See Example 6-7)**

Color Chords are a way of combining *four dominant seventh chords.* **(See Example 6-5)** The roots of these dominant sevenths are a minor third apart, which describes the notes of a diminished seventh chord. When the notes of these dominants are combined, *all the notes in a diminished scale are present.* For instance, the combination of B Flat, D Flat, E, and G, can be combined to contain all the notes of a B, D, F, or A Flat Diminished Scale (they are all the same scale). **(See Example 6-8)**

EXAMPLE 6-5 COLOR CHORD COMBINATIONS

1) B♭	D♭	E	G
2) B	D	F	A♭
3) C	E♭	G♭	A

48. COLOR CHORD EXERCISE

1) Take each color chord combination in turn and experiment with combining the sevenths. For example, mix a D Flat7 with a G7; and a B Flat7 with an E7. Try all combinations of this color group as chords and arpeggios. Try playing two notes from, let's say, a B Flat7, the A Flat and B Flat in the left hand and a G7 in the right hand as an arpeggio up the piano.

2) Try playing the Modal Exercise from the chapter on Beginning Improv using the Color Chords.

3) When playing a ballad, add in color combinations whenever you have a dominant chord. You can also play with color chords as substitutions. Note that one of the color chord combinations is the tritone substitution. This is also a good modulation device.

4) It is also possible to think in terms of color chords when you are soloing. This works great when you are playing over any dominant or diminished chord. Keep in mind that a lot of the *passing chords* that you can use to move between one chord and another can be a diminished chord. This opens up fresh possibilities.

5) Listen to Debussy to hear many examples of color chords.

6) Practice the Diminished Exercise in all keys. **(See Example 6-9)**

EXAMPLE 6-6   HALF/WHOLE AND WHOLE/ HALF DIMINISHED SCALES

1.

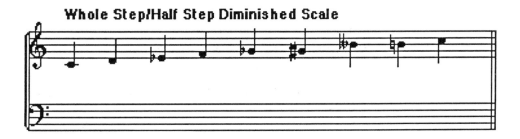

2.   C#Dim⁷   Half Step/Whole Step Diminished Scale

Whole Step/Half Step Diminished Scale

3.   D Dim⁷   Half Step/Whole Step Diminished Scale

Whole Step/Half Step Diminished Scale

EXAMPLE 6-7   DIMINISHED SCALE AND CHORDS

Tritone Sub.

EXAMPLE 6-8   COLOR CHORDS AND DIMINISHED SCALE

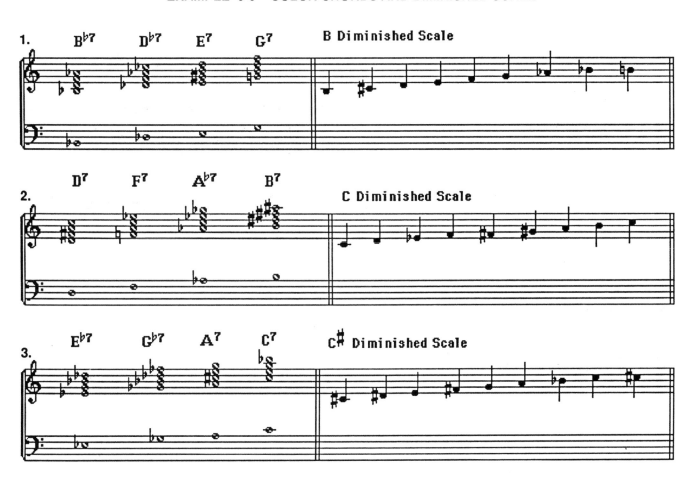

EXAMPLE 6-9   DIMINISHED SCALE EXERCISE

49. ADVANCED CHORD VOICINGS AND SCALES

In the world of jazz, a jazz player almost never plays a chord in the root position, in thirds stacked up the chord. This is one of the main confusions in the mind of the classical player, because in music school, they were always taught chords in this way. Another major confusion is created by thinking of chords from the bottom of the chord up to the top. Jazz players, arrangers and composers most often think of a chord from the top of the chord down. They do this for a logical reason, the melody of the chord voicing is on the top. In other words, *think of chords in a melodic way.*

When I am comping behind an instrumental soloist or a vocalist, I am voicing my comping chords so that they are playing certain counter-melodies against what the soloist is playing. Incidentally, it is also as important to *think of melodies in a harmonic way.* This will be covered later in this chapter.

Secondly, as expressed before, chords are not to be thought of as solid, concrete entities. Try to de-emphasize naming chords in their exact inversions. Instead, think of chords as two or more notes out of a Mode or Scale. There are many many ways to construct scales, and with each construct there are many combinations of chords. It is fun, just to create your own scales and then experiment with many combinations of chordal possibilities. This is very intuitive and musical, because you are working directly with sounds and not simply labels of chord names.

In other words, scales and chords are totally intertwined. If you have a scale, you can make many many chords out of that scale. Also, if you have a chord, you can fill in notes of your own choice between the notes of that chord, and in so doing, make up your own scale. Remember, that with each scale, you can create modes by starting on any note in that scale.

One of the best ways to get out of the doldrums of hearing the same type of improvisation, is to come up with fresh harmonic sounds. This means chords into scales, and/or scales into chords. Again, try not to get too deep into labeling everything that you do, it is better to simply experience it freshly. If you want, put emotional labels on scales and chords, rather than numbers. Call one scale or chord, happy and another sad, whatever. This will definitely add new spice to your playing.

Also it is possible to reharmonize entire tunes with new chord types. Of course, this has to be done with great discretion, but you can come up with many new ideas this way. Every so often, *Keyboard Magazine* invites a number of composers to come up with special arrangements of a tune like *"Greensleeves"*. It is always fun to see how many ways a tune can be re-harmonized and how different it makes the tune feel.

The point is, don't worry too much about rules, let your ears and inner musicianship be your guide. The main rule is to clearly have a *goal* in what you are writing. Then place the harmonies in the *context* of that goal. If you are writing a simple Country Western tune, do not use Stravinsky-like harmonies!

I am going to present several exercises to help open your ears to new harmonies. We tend to hang on to old harmonic concepts - and get bored as a result. The point is to become friends with new harmonies. Live with them until you will musically speak with these harmonies. Remember, music is a language and language must be part of us. Therefore, enjoy these mental games, and enjoy the future results. Try not to have too many preconceptions at this point. Just have fun and see what happens. Good Luck.

50. VOICINGS

It is more important to *know how to find your own voicings* than to have someone tell you supposed "hip" voicings because if you have certain voicings which are elevated above others in importance, you, most assuredly, will use them over and over. In other words, you will probably sound like everyone else. As a classical player, you have a wide harmonic language already available in your subconscious from the compositions that you have been playing for many years. You want to be an original and to bring all your experience to your jazz.

I like the idea of finding a sound, call it a chord or voicing first, then finding a purpose for it later. In other words, it is fun to sit at the piano, let you hands find a chordal sound that you like. Then you have to analyze it in terms of its intervalic content. Here is an example: The following chord or voicing is a sound commonly found in jazz. Some players call it the "So What" chord because it is used in a jazz tune by the same name. Just look at the chord, do not worry about its name or function. Do not try to figure out its root. Just analyze the chord as an intervallic structure. In this case, it stacks two perfect fourths and a third on top. Let's call it **4-4-4-3.** **(See Example 6-10)**

EXAMPLE 6-10   4-4-4-3 VOICING (SO WHAT CHORD)

Let's start by playing this voicing up and down chromatically. Think of it in its intervals. Let it float, do not worry about it's root. Then, play this voicing all over the piano, from very low to very high. Certainly, you will like some sounds, and others will not be pleasant to you. The main idea is to *experience* this particular sound.

Then start playing melodies using only this voicing. Even a simple nursery rhyme will do. **(See Example 6-11)** Play the voicing in many melodies and in all keys of the original melody. Try playing up a major scale with this voicing. The top note of the voicing plays the major scale. **(See Example 6-12).**

It has been my observation that if you play a voicing enough times and in enough ways, it will find its way into your piano stylings. The subconscious will automatically start using it as part of your languange. If you hear **Chick Corea** or **Keith Jarrett** play harmonies which you do not understand, remember that those harmonies are understandable to their subconscious. That is why they are able to use those harmonic structures so freely.

After you have familiarized yourself with the voicing, then you might want to analyze it in terms of the possible scales or modes that it belongs to and what possible roots can be played with it. In the case of quartal harmony, the harmonic structure is usually vague and many roots can be applied to it. The "So What" voicing can sound well in a major scale context; a mixolydian mode context; or a minor context. It's a handy chord to use for comping. In general, it is a more modern sound to us than tertial harmony (chords in thirds).

Here are some commonly used voicings.

Notice that some use perfect fourth intervals and some use the tritone or augmented fourth. It is recommended that you learn just one chord at a time. Of course, find your *own* chords and learn them. I have deliberately not included the roots. Play up the chromatic scale and you will find the roots which work. **(See Example 6-13)**

EXAMPLE 6-11 - MELODY HARMONIZED WITH ONE VOICING

EXAMPLE 6-12 MAJOR SCALE PLAYED WITH ONE VOICING

EXAMPLE 6-13   SOME VOICINGS

51. CHORD STRUCTURES

One of my favorite ways to learn a new scale or mode, is to play the game, *Chord Structures*. Chord structures is deceptively simple. But I know first hand in my own experience that it works. This is a very good way to get to know any scale or mode inside out. I highly recommend practicing this with all scales that you know, and want to learn.

We will start with the Major Scale. Always start in the key of "C" because it is easier to look down at the keyboard and see the structures. Choose a structure, let's say fingers 1,2,5 in the right hand. If you hold that structure, you can play up and down the scale using 1, 2, and 5. The intervals will slightly change as you move up the Major Scale. Now comes the hard part, *play this in all keys.*

Practice this exercise in any structure of your choice. Make sure that you play in all keys. Next, break up the structures. Play the structures in single notes, in any order. This will greatly help your modal improv. **(See Example 6-14)**

EXAMPLE 6-14   CHORD STRUCTURES

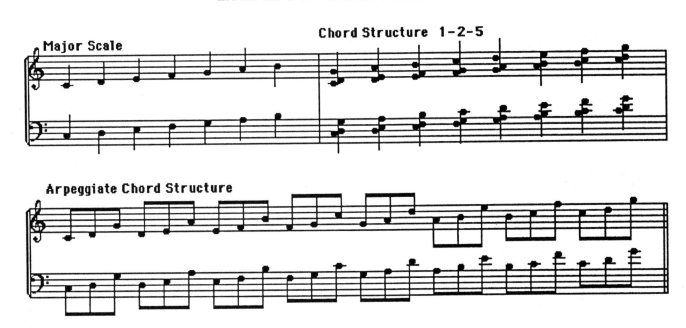

52. SCALE CONSTRUCTION

It is highly recommended that you experiment with constructing your own scales. Remember that any scale that you construct will have its own modes. The modes offer further exploration. Also each scale that you construct will have its own chords and chord voicings. The main point is to become completely familiar with your scales so that you can freely compose and improvise with them.

53. TETRACHORDS

Tetrachords are four note scale fragments. Any four continuous notes can actually be construed as a tetrachord. First find a tetrachord of your choice. Note the interval relationship between the notes. Now play your new tetrachord in all keys. Next try combining tetrachords. They may be the same tetrachord, let's say one half step apart, or can be a combination of two or three different tetrachords. These combinations have the possibilities of creating many new scales. Once you have your new scale, then you also have modes and chordal structures from that scale. **(See Example 6-15)**

54. PENTATONIC SCALES

The Pentatonics are five-note scale fragments. They are often used in today's jazz and rock. It is particularly fun and creative to create your own Pentatonics. Here are some examples: **(See Example 6-16)**

55. WHOLE TONE SCALES

The Whole Tone Scale is a very simple scale because it is an *equal distant scale*. All the *six* steps are whole steps. There are 12 tones in the Chromatic Scale. This means that there are two different Whole Tone Scales. These scales are used for Augmented Chords with a flatted seventh. **(See Example 6-17)**

56. MELODIC MINOR SCALE

After you have thoroughly learned and assimilated the Major Scale and its modes, and the Diminished Scale, the next scale to master is the Melodic Minor. The Melodic Minor will give you a very current jazz sound. Many of today's current jazz musicians use this scale to a great extent. It will definitely modernize your sound.

As with all of the other scales, you must start slowly and deliberately to integrate this sound into your arrangements and soloing. Use the Modal Improv exercise to develop modal arrangements. Make up some Groove Tunes which use this scale. Practice the Chord Structures exercise. Listen for this sound in your jazz records. Definitely practice in all keys. **(See Exercise 6-18)**

57. HARMONIC MINOR MODES

The Harmonic Minor Scale and its modes are also used in today's contemporary jazz. This scale and its modes are not used as often as as the Major and Melodic Minor, however you will find a wealth of ideas by learning this scale and its modes. **(See Example 6-19)**

58. SCALE EXERCISES

1) The following exercise is similar to the Modal Exercise and also the Stop on the Chord Exercise. Pick any scale or mode. First, develop a rhythm by patting on your lap. Choose two of the same modes, each in a different key, or change the scales or modes. Then play and play developing scale or mode #1 and then switch to scale or mode #2. You will be surprised at how easy it is to compose entire compositions in this way. Of course, you can use any amount of scales that you wish. Change the rhythms as often as you wish.

2) Take any beautiful ballad, such as "Here's that Rainy Day"; or "But Beautiful", or "Lover Man" etc. Chart out the tune in your notebook. Note all the places that you can us the Tritone Substitution. Then have fun using the Stop on the Chord Exercise. Try to experiment using all the scales and modes. This will, of course, change the type of chord. In some cases, this will mean that you have to change the melody. Keep trying and have fun. Of course, play the ballad *in all keys.*

3) Play with rhythms and time signatures. If, for instance the tune is in 4/4, try it in 3/4 or whatever. If the tune is a ballad, try playing it as an up tune, or perhaps a Latin.

4) Play your beautiful ballad by first playing an arrangement which defines the melody. Then start soloing on the next choruses. Try the continuous stream of notes to start, then start adding phrasing and space. Play chorus after chorus until you really know the tune and start building your confidence in your ability to improvise. Remember, try to prehear what you are playing. At first, maybe you will hear only 50% of the notes, but soon you will be hearing 100%. Also try

singing along with your playing.

5) Play along with the Aebersold Records.

6) Buy written arrangements by excellent pianists such as **George Shearing, Bill Evans and Oscar Peterson**. Experiment with these arrangements. You do not have to play them note for note. If in fact, you can use just part of an arrangement and fill in your own ideas. *For the most part, stay away from sheet music arrangements.*

7) Study improv with a teacher who is a good improviser. He or she will teach you a great deal from his or her experience.

8) Most importantly, try to find a playing situation. It is very important that you play with other musicians and for an audience.

EXAMPLE 6-15 SOME TETRACHORDS

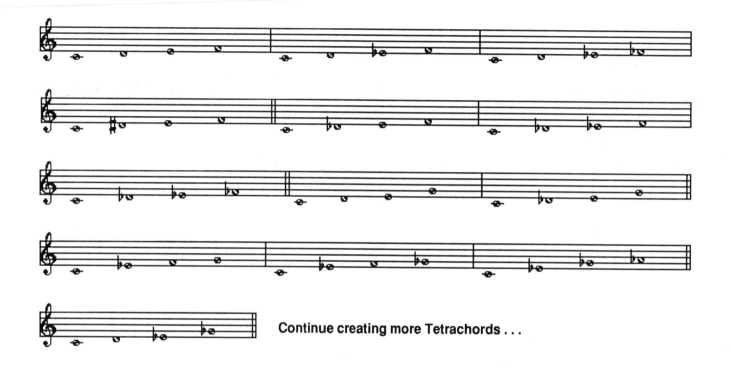

Continue creating more Tetrachords . . .

EXAMPLE 6-16 SOME PENTATONICS

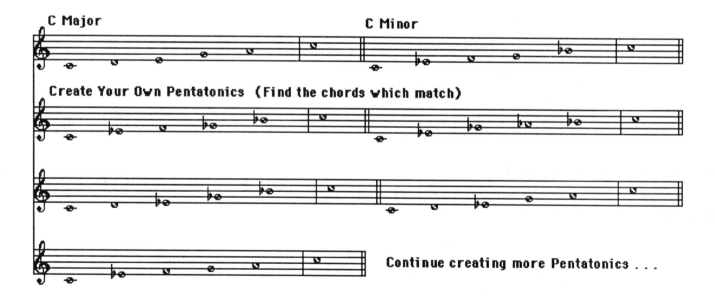

C Major

C Minor

Create Your Own Pentatonics (Find the chords which match)

Continue creating more Pentatonics . . .

EXAMPLE 6-17   WHOLE TONE SCALES

EXAMPLE 6-18   MELODIC MINOR MODES

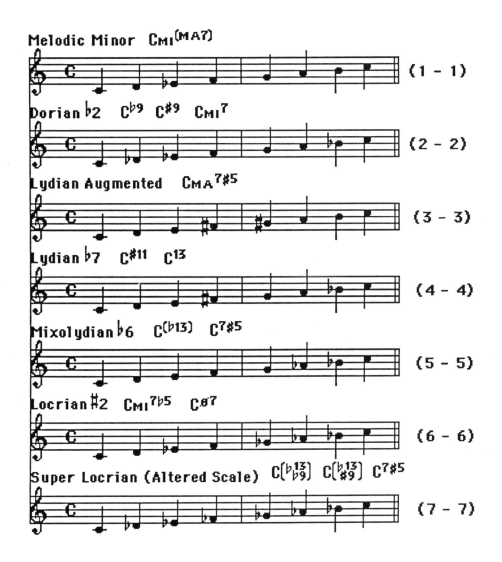

EXAMPLE 6-19   HARMONIC MINOR MODES

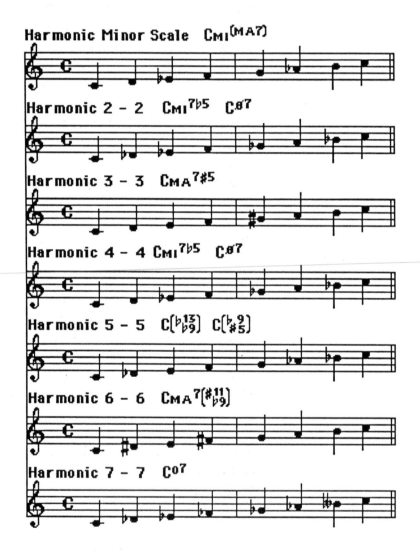

59. CHORD ALTERATIONS, EXTENSIONS, AND TONALITIES

One of the favorite ways a jazz player personalizes an arrangement or an improvisation, is to alter the *type* of chord. This is different from substitutions because you are not altering the root of the chord,or exchanging one chord for another, however, you are tinkering with the *coloration* of the chord.

Let's say that a major chord which comes from the Major Scale, sounds "yellow". By changing the chord to a minor seventh flat five (also known as a Half Diminished), we are feeling the Locrian Mode or the Locrian sharp 2 mode. Now, for example's sake, let's imagine that the color has changed from "yellow" to "magenta" (purely speculative of course). This does show the tie in between chords and scales or modes, or what I like to term, *"Tonality"*.

Whenever I read a chord in a fake book, I think "tonality". This allows me a great deal of freedom to voice chords and to create melodies which work with that tonality. Therefore, a tune is literally "swimming" in a constantly shifting tonal "sea". Every time we flat a ninth or sharp a fourth, we change the scale. This in turn, entirely changes the feeling of the music.

It is common for a jazz player to totally alter the feeling of a tune through these kinds of chord/scale alterations. If you practice the Modal Exercise or "Stop on the Chord", you can experience the fun of changing chords and tonalities.

The following example will show you some possible alterations. Consult with the Examples on Major Scale Modes, the Melodic Minor Modes, the Harmonic Minor Modes, the Whole Tone Scale, the Diminished Scale and the Pentatonic Scales to find which Tonality matches the chord. Remember, you can also *make up your own Tonalities.* Have fun and experiment.

Notice that the chord alterations have been set up off of the II, V, I exercise. You can practice these alterations by playing the II, V, I exercise altering any combination of the II, V, and/or I. You can also practice playing the chords in the left hand and improvising over the chords in the right hand. To do this, you will have to discover which tonalities or scales fit the alterations. You can practice "Stop on the Chord" if it will help you to become familiar with the tonalities.

Finally, insert these alterations into your arrangements and improvisations. There is a new world of sound and emotion to discover. Keep at it! **(See Examples 20, 21, and 22)**

60. SCALES FROM CHORDS

One creative way to construct a scale is to play a chord, *any* chord. Then, simply fill in the notes between the chord tones. There will be several note selections available to you and you can try them all. Once you have discovered your "new" scale, write it out and especially note the intervals from note to note. This will enable you to *play the scale in all keys.* You might try Chord Structures using your scale and also might try creating melodic triads out of the new scale.

When you are improvising with solo lines, you can also come up with some instantaneous scales by filling in the notes between the chord tones.

EXAMPLE 6-20   SOME POSSIBLE ALTERATIONS OF THE II MINOR CHORD

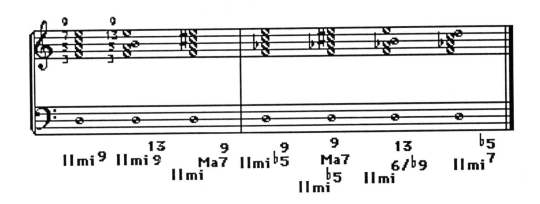

EXAMPLE 6-21   SOME POSSIBLE EXTENSIONS OF THE V DOMINANT CHORD

EXAMPLE 6-22 SOME POSSIBLE EXTENSIONS OF THE I CHORD (MAJOR, MINOR, AUG. & DIM.)

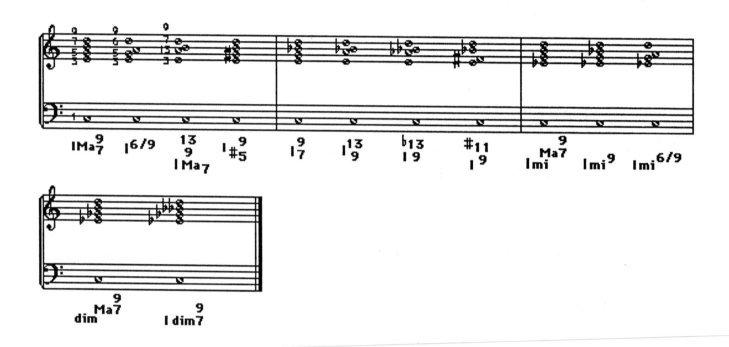

Advanced Theory - Review

CHORD SUBSTITUTIONS

1)   Do you understand the basis of the *Tritone Sub-stitution*? **(Section 45, Page 183 & Example 6-1, Page 184)**

Completed: Date_____

2)   Have you practiced the *basic I, VI, II, V Turnaround in all keys*? **(Example 6-2, Page 185)**

Completed: Date_____

3)   Have you practiced the *Dominant I, VI, II, V Turnaround in* all keys? **(Example 6-3, Page 186)**

Completed: Date_____

3)   Here's a big one! Have you practiced the *variations of the Tritone Substution in all keys*? This will take a long time. **(Example 6-4, Page 187)**

Completed: Date_____

4)   Can you *solo* over the variations of the Tritone Substitution? Use the II, V, I as a basis for improvisation. Also use the Modal Improv.

Completed: Date_____

DIMINISHED SCALE

5)   Can you play the three *Diminished Scales* with either hand and with both hands? **(Example 6-6, Pages 191 and 192)**

Completed: Date_____

6)   Do you know the *Color Chord "Families"*? **(Example 6-5, Page 190 & Example 6-8, Page 193)**

Completed: Date_____

7)   Have you mastered the *Color Chord Exercise*? **(Section 48, Pages 190 & 191)**

Completed: Date_____

8) Can you play the *Diminished Scale Exercise*? **(Example 6-9, Page 194)**

Completed: Date_____

9) Can you play some Modal Improvisations using the Diminished Scales and Color Chords?

Completed: Date_____

10) Can you insert the diminished scale into your improvisation on *Eliza*?

Completed: Date_____

ADVANCED CHORD VOICINGS

11) Have you learned the *"So What"* chord? Can you play it up and down the Major Scale? Can you play it as a melody of a tune? **(Examples 6-10, 6-11 & 6-12, Pages 197 - 198)**

Completed: Date_____

12) Can you do the above exercise using **Example 6-13, Page 200** and also *make up your own Advanced Chord Voicings*? This will take a long time.

Completed: Date_____

13) Do you see these voicings entering into your improvisations and comping on tunes?

Completed: Date_____

CHORD STRUCTURES

14) Have you played the Chord Structures Exercise using different intervals? Can you play these structures in all keys? **(Example 6-14, Page 201)**

Completed: Date_____

15) Have you tried to arpeggiate the structures in different melodic order? **(Example 6-14, Page 201)**

Completed: Date_____

SCALE CONSTRUCTION

16) Have you tried to *construct* different Tetra-chords? Can you play them in all keys? **(Example 6-15, Page 206)**

Completed: Date_____

17) Have you tried to *combine Tetrachords* to create new scales?

Completed: Date_____

PENTATONIC SCALES

18) Have you tried to *construct* different *Pentatonic Scales*? Can you play them in all keys? **(Example 6-16, Page 206)**

Completed: Date_____

19) Have you tried to *combine Pentatonic Scales* to create new scales?

Completed: Date_____

WHOLE TONE SCALES

20) Have you learned the two Whole Tone Scales? Can you use them in improvisation? **(Example 6-17, Page 207)**

Completed: Date_____

MELODIC MINOR SCALE

21) Have you thoroughly learned the *Melodic Minor Scales* in all keys? This will take a long time. **(Example 6-18, Page 207)**

Completed: Date_____

22) Have you explored all the *Modes of the Melodic Minor* and the Chords that they match? **(Example 6-18, Page 207)**

Completed: Date_____

23) Have you found places in *tunes* which use the Melodic Minor Scale and Modes and practiced *"Stop on the Chord"*?

Completed: Date_____

24) Have you practiced *Chord Structures* using the Melodic Minor Scale?

Completed: Date_____

HARMONIC MINOR SCALE

25) Have you explored all the *Modes of the Harmonic Minor* and the Chords that they match? This will take a long time **Example 6-19, Page 208)**

Completed: Date_____

26) Have you found places in *tunes* which use the Harmonic Minor Scale and Modes and practiced *"Stop on the Chord"*?

Completed: Date_____

27) Have you practiced *Chord Structures* using the Harmonic Minor Scale?

Completed: Date_____

CHORD ALTERATIONS AND TONALITIES

28) Have you explored all the *Chord Alterations and Tonalities* by using the II, V, I Exercise. Can you play them in all keys and inversions? This *will* take a long time. **(Examples 6-20, 21,22, Pages 211 & 212)**

Completed: Date_____

29) Have you tried to use these alterations and tonalities in the tunes in which you are working?

Completed: Date_____

SCALES FROM CHORDS

30) Have you experimented with creating scales from any chords of your own construction? Have you catalogued your favorites in your workbook?

Completed: Date_____

31) Have you tried to create modal improvisations using these chords and scales?

Completed: Date_____

Note:

I hope this Chapter hasn't worn you out. This represents the ongoing nature of the study of music in general and jazz in particular. As we continue, we add new concepts and music theories into our subconscious and through the process of language begin to express ourselves. It is fun to develop this self expression. Carry on . . .

Final Thoughts

I'm sure you will agree that this book is not easy. The main difficulty lies with the assimilation of what I feel is basic information which must reside in your subconscious. Improvisation by its very nature is hard to teach because each person will want to improvise in his own way. The main job of this book is to get you started and to give you the means to keep on going, until you are happy with the results.

Therefore, it is my hope that you do not give up. Given the years that you have spent studying the piano, to be able to interpret beautiful and profound music, should bear good fruit for you if you keep trying. Remember the analogy that "music is a language" and keep trying to speak music.

Improvisation does not happen in a void, and it is highly advised that you spend a great deal of time listening to the kind of music that you want to improvise. A great deal of emphasis in this book is placed on your listening critically and then trying to copy the *style* and *phrasing* of the improviser. Also, it would be very helpful if you had an opportunity to play for others, either in a professional situation or in a practice band. It is important to have the constant "conversation" between other musicians in the band and also with the audience.

Also, it would be good for you to try to compose music also. Composition demands more commitment and more depth of thought than improvisation and you will develop into your own style this way. I fervently hope that you will try new things. Experiment. Rules and labels get in the way of creativity. Just try to experience your improvisations and compositions without judgment.

This book purposely did not present you with composed improvisations. The reason was that you can already find many jazz arrangements in books written for that purpose. Also, you are encouraged to purchase a jazz *fake book*, such as the "Real Book" as a source of tunes. Also, the **Jamey Aebersold** record series is a marvelous way to learn new tunes. Look primarily for the records which contain standards. Then after awhile, branch out into the jazz tunes. The records not only teach you the melody and chord changes of the tunes but give you unlimited practice at soloing with a rhythm section. Start a collection of your memorized tunes in your workbook so that if you go on a job or sit in a jam session, you will know the tunes that you can play comfortably.

Keep on filling your workbook with tunes and ideas. You will watch it grow. Also you will develop confidence as your knowledge grows.

THE VIDEO

The video (available soon) which is the companion for this book will help you greatly because you can see and hear demonstrations of the written word. The study of improvisation really needs a teacher because so much has to be demonstrated. Study the video examples carefully and really try to get into the *thinking* of the improviser.

FUTURE BOOKS

I am also currently working on a series of supplements to this book. The emphasis will be on learning to play specific styles. If you are interested in being notified about these and other publications and recordings, please write me at **Musicmann, P.O. Box 1522, Cupertino, CA 95015-1522** or call **(408) 996-8937.** I am always interested in your questions and suggestions. I am also available for teaching private lessons and master classes in jazz improvisation.

Finally, and most importantly, this book is dedicated to the enjoyment of music. Good luck, and keep trying!

Further Study

Adler, Wilfred
Piano Improvising, Pacific, MO: Mel Bay Publications, 1977.

Aebersold, Jamey.
A New Approach to Jazz Improvisation (Records), New Albany, IN: Jamey
Aebersold, 1978.

Baker, David.
Techniques of Improvisation Vols. 1 - 4, Chicago, Ill: Maher Publications,
1971.

Baker, David.
Advanced Improvisation, Chicago, Ill: Maher Publications, 1974.

Bellson, Louis.
Modern Reading Text in 4/4, New York: Henry Adler, Inc., 1963.

Bishop, Walter.
A Study in Fourths, NY: Caldon Publishing Co., 1976.

Burswold, Lee
Practice Routines: Chords in Fourths, Extended Dominants and Augmented
Elevenths, Lebanon, In: Studio 224, Studio P/R, Inc., 1983.

Burswold, Lee.
Topics in Jazz Piano Improvisation, Lebanon, In: Studio 224, Studio P/R, Inc.,
1980.

Carubia, Mike.
The Sound of Improvisation, Port Washington, NY: Alfred Publishing, Co., Inc.,
1976.

Coker, Jerry, Jimmy Casale, Gary Campbell, & Jerry Greene.
Patterns for Jazz, Lebanon, In: Studio 224, Studio P/R, Inc., 1977.

Coker, Jerry.
Figure Reading Series, Rhythmic Studies of Today's Music, Miami, Fl: Studio 224., 1987.

Coker, Jerry.
Complete Method for Improvisation. Lebanon, IN: Studo P/R, Inc., 1980.

Coker, Jerry.
Improvising Jazz, Englewood Cliffs, NJ: Prentice-Hall, 1964.

Cortot, Alfred.
Rational Principles of Pianoforte Technique. Paris: Editions Salabert, 1930.

Dallin, Leo.
Techniques of Twentieth Century Composition. 2nd ed. Dubuque, Iowa: Wm. C. Brown Co. Publishers, 1964

Giesking, Walter and Carl Leimer.
Piano Technique, NY: Dover Publications., 1972.

Gillespie, Dizzy.
To Be or not to Bop, Garden City, NY: Doubleday and Co., Inc., 1979.

Gold, Arthur and Robert Fizdale.
Hanon Revisited, Contemporary Piano Exercises. New York: G. Schirmer, Inc.,1968.

Green, Barry and W. Timothy Gallwey.
The Inner Game of Music, Garden City, NY: Anchor Press, Doubleday, 1986.

Grove, Dick
Arranging Concepts, Complete. Studio City, CA: Dick Grove Publications, 1972.

Grove, Dick.
Modern Harmonic Relationships, Studio City, CA: Dick Grove Publications, 1977

Grove, Dick.
Advanced Modern Harmony, Studio City, CA: Dick Grove Publications, 1983

Grove, Dick.
Fundamentals of Modern Harmony, Studio City, CA: Dick Grove Publications, 1977

Haerle, Dan .
Jazz Improvisation for Keyboard Players, Lebanon, In: Studio 224, Studio P/R, Inc., 1978.

Haerle, Dan.
Jazz/Rock Voicings for the Contemporary Keyboard Player, Lebanon, In: Studio 224, Studio P/R, Inc., 1974.

Hagen, Earle.
Scoring for Films, New York: E. D. J. Music, Inc., 1971.

Hanon, C.L.
The Virtuoso Pianist in 60 Exercises. New York: G. Schirmer, Inc., 1900.

Hindemith, Paul.
The Craft of Musical Composition. New York: Associated Music Publishers, 1941.

Holcombe, Bill.
Creative Arranging at the Piano, West Trenton, NJ: Musicians Publications, 1984.

Joyce, Jimmy.
A Guide to Writing Vocal Arrangements, Santa Monica, CA: First Place Music Pub., Inc., 1972

Kasha, Al, and Joel Hirschhorn.
If They Ask You, You can Write a Song. New York: Simon and Schuster, 1979

Keyboard Magazine.
Cupertino, CA, GPI Publications.

Lloyd, Ruth and Norman
Creative Keyboard Musicianship. New York: Dodd, Mead & Co., 1975.

Lyons, Len.
The Great Jazz Pianists, NY: Quill, 1983.

Mason, Thom David.
Ear Training for the Improviser, A Total Approach. Studio City, CA: Dick Grove Pub. 1981.

Matthay, Tobias.
Musical Interpretation, Boston, MA: Boston Music Co. 1913.

Mehegan, John
Touch and Rhythm Techniques for the Jazz Pianist, New York: Sam Fox Pub lishing Co., 1962.

Mehegan, John.
Jazz Improvisation Vol. 1 - 4. New York: Watson-Guptill Publications, 1962.

Most, Sam.
Metamorphosis, Transformation of the Jazz Solo, Tustin, CA.: Professional Music Products, Inc.,1980.

Nelson, Oliver
Patterns for Improvisation, Los Angeles, CA: Noslen Music Co., 1966.

Niehaus, Lennie.
Concepts in Jazz, Winona, MN: Hal Leonard Publishing Corp., 1981.

Novello, John.
The Contemporary Keyboardist. Toluca Lake, CA: Source Productions, 1986.

Oestereich, James and Earl Pennington
Improvising and Arranging on the Keyboard. New Jersey: Prentice-Hall, Inc., 1981.

Pace, Robert
Music for Piano. New York: Lee Roberts Music Publications, Inc., 1962

Persichetti, Vincent.
Twentieth Century Harmony, NY: W. W. Norton & Co., 1961.

Piston, Walter.
Harmony. New York: W. W. Norton & Co., 1969

Ricker, Ramon.
New Concepts in Linear Improvisation, Lebanon, In: Studio 224, Studio P/R, Inc., 1977.

Ricker, Ramon.
Pentatonic Scales for Jazz Improvisations, Lebanon, In: Studio 224, Studio
   P/R, Inc., 1975.
Ricker, Ramon.
Technique Development in Fourths for Jazz Improvisation, Lebanon, In: Studio
   224, Studio P/R, Inc., 1976.

Roemer, Clinton.
The Art of Music Copying, Sherman Oaks, CA: Roerick Music Co., 1973.

Russell, George.
The Lydian Chromatic Concept of Tonal Organization. New York: Concept Pub.
   Co.

Russo, William.
Jazz Composition and Orchestration. London: University of Chicago Press,
   1968.

Shemel, Sidney, and M. William Krasilovsky.
This Business of Music. New York: Billboard Publications, 1977.

Slonimsky, Nicolas.
Thesaurus of Scales and Melodic Patterns. New York: Charles Scribner's
   Sons. 1947.

Smith, Leland.
Handbook of Harmonic Analysis, Stanford University, CA: Leland Smith, 1963.